Dear reader: Befc

I'd like to offer you a ...

It's a free download of our recent report on Influence.

In this one-of-a-kind report, find out how your peers define "influence"

This e-book contains the thoughts and opinions of almost 100 professionals and executives all over the world and important insights you might find useful about your own influence.

Just go to this link, and it's yours.

http://www.ezinfluence.com/free-report/

PRAISE FOR *A SWIFT KICK IN THE CAN'TS*

"Elaina Zuker has written a clear, concise and helpful book on moving out of stagnation to setting and reaching your goals. She has some smart ideas on peer mentoring and easy to use suggestions for identifying skills and goal setting. The book is written in accessible and easily understandable language – as exemplified by the title itself."

—*Dr. Leslie Faerstein*

"A QUICK READ FOR GOAL ORIENTED SUCCESS! This is "it" if you are looking for a well-focused and concisely defined quick and lively read. You will easily connect to your own personal needs and goals as you strive for the success you deserve. Go for it!!!!!"

—*Emily Rosen*

"This informative business book provides the reader with some unique ideas for increasing your business success through the sharing of skills...it is a skills bartering system that can be of huge benefit to small business owners and start ups. Barter is ages old and has been used in many different ways throughout the ages. Elaina's research and the input of colleagues, offers the reader some great ideas on how to leverage your skills in order to gain some that you may not have or wish to learn.

Any business owner will find this approach worth the read and possibly worth exploring to improve outcomes and even bottom lines!"

—*Sandy Chernoff*

"I recommend this book to anyone wants to advance their career and build lasting relationships with smart and interesting people."

—*Molly Sutherland*

"Elaina has written another practical and powerful book to help get better results in the business world. As an owner/operator business, I sometimes wish I could have a coach or a mentor by my side to guide me, offer me the skills I don't have and motivate me to get going on my next project or make that difficult phone call.

A Swift Kick in the Can'ts does just that – and a lot more. I especially liked the "Skills Inventory", the Goal Setting exercises and the "how to" details she provides. I've already started on my search for a Peer Mentor."

—*Marcia*

"I read it from cover to cover and just loved it. It was interesting, factual and easy to grasp. Honestly it gave ME a kick in the can'ts. In my over thirty-year real estate career I have worked in partnerships and "mentoring" relationships with many other professionals and to mutual benefit. For some of them it would have been useful to have had Elaina's model and "contract" ideas to clarify those relationships!"

—*Janet Gifford*

"I read *A Swift Kick in the Can'ts* after hearing Elaina Zuker speak at a workshop in New York City. The idea of peer mentoring was new to me. This book is a breeze with a thought provoking premise . Elaina points out that as we intuitively and organically move more and more towards a sharing economy, the individualistic "by my bootstraps" ideology/myth has run its course and we are starting to be more honest and explicit about the fact that we rely on a network of friends and contacts for our successes..."

—*Shindy Johnson*

A Swift Kick in The Can'ts

The New Peer Mentor Model for Success Now

Elaina Zuker

Cover design by Tatiana Villa
Interior formatting by Veronica Yager

ISBN: 978-1-62967-073-7
Library of Congress Control Number: 2016909522

to Nadav – the spirit of generosity

Contents

Introduction

If you want to increase your productivity, enhance your earning power, achieve your goals, and reach more overall success in your life (whether measured in money, expertise, or relationships), then read on. Peer Mentoring™ is a system in which two people agree to support each other based on complementary skills and needs, and the partners create a 'contract.' The purpose of this process is to create a productively paired 'buddy system' to help both of you achieve your individual goals.

There have been numerous books and articles about mentoring, finding someone senior to you in your field who will help, advise, consult, and coach you to realize your potential. Having a mentor (if you can find one) can definitely be an asset to you and your career. Lately, we hear a lot about the power of networking in all its formats, such as 'live' networking - going to events, collecting business cards, and then following up on those contacts. Of course, we also have cyber networking thanks to Facebook, Twitter, and the most business-related platform, LinkedIn. The end goal is finding the contacts who will be helpful to you or your business. Peer Mentoring is a combination or confluence of these two trends (networking and mentoring), regardless of the business or career you're engaged in.

I first discovered the idea of Peer Mentoring when I began using it for myself. I met another woman consultant who had many of the skills, experiences, and contacts that I lacked. I had some of the resources and talents she needed. We formed a contract with each other in which we made very clear statements of our separate goals, and then we made clear written commitments to support each other in achieving those goals. Some of this support came from teaching each other the skills the other needed, sharing our contacts, educating each other in areas where we needed more information, and, most importantly, just knowing that we each had a buddy rooting for us. We called it a "loving kick in the can'ts".

Our mutual support system was so effective that we found that we had each achieved our one-year goals after only a few months. During this period, we met once a week, reviewed our short-term and long-term goals, discussed how effectively we were spending our time, and took turns instructing each other on subjects in which one of us wanted more knowledge. We were so amazed by our success that we decided to teach this process to others. Now, thousands of people all over the country have learned the process and are actively forming Peer-Mentor pairs to help each other to be more successful.

Peer Mentoring is a process through which people identify their own resources and those of others and then create specific strategies for mutual goal achievement. It is a new adaptation of the age-old concept of reciprocity practiced by all cultures. Usual reciprocal practices are implicit, whereas the Peer-Mentor contract makes the agreements explicit. The participants barter resources (skills, contacts, technical expertise, advice, counseling, criticism, etc.) with each other as needed. That idea alone sets it apart from the plethora of 'How To Succeed' theories. This model encourages the development and organization of one's readily available resources – personal, business, and social – and is based on mutual support. It is different from the "I can do it myself through gritted teeth" attitude, which I believe most people find extremely difficult in practice. The Peer-Mentoring technique challenges the myth that isolation is a necessary companion of success.

THE PEER MENTOR SYSTEM IS AN UNUSUAL RELATIONSHIP WHOSE TIME HAS COME

Peer-Mentoring is based on a complementary relationship that offers maximum benefit for both its participants. The value in these exchanges is that they are not necessarily about friendship, having a good time together, or being similar. In fact, the agreements often work better when there are differences – complementarities – between the two partners. Each peer is, then, both the mentor *and* the protégé. Complementary skills and needs form the basis of this system of pairing. The pair becomes a relationship for support, guidance, and resource-sharing to achieve each individual's goals.

Over several decades in my work as a management consultant, I have run seminars and workshops all over the U.S. and internationally with groups of people from those in top management positions to secretaries on topics as varied as Writing Skills, Time Management, Leadership, and Team Building. At the end of the workshop on any of these topics, we organize the participants into complementary pairs, then explain how to use the Peer-Mentor process to reinforce what has been taught. The partners are instructed to spell out clearly what they want and are prepared to offer each other and put all of these details in writing. Thousands of workshop participants have asked me for further advice on how they can adapt the technique and methods for implementing it in their daily lives. The process' success has proven effective in many settings: at the manager, staff, and professional level and in schools, colleges, and non-profit groups.

The Peer-Mentor relationship is not wishful thinking. It is structured around a written contract between two people which specifies, in detail, what goals each person has, what strategies she will use to achieve them, the targets, timeframes, and measures, metrics, and indicators by which she will know when the goals have been reached. The operative word is "peer," someone at one's own level and not necessarily a senior or superior person in rank or position. The role of the Peer-Mentor is to keep the other on target, to help push through the fears, internal blocks, and procrastination – to believe in the other even when she does not believe in herself.

Each participant must agree to both receive and provide the support, counsel, sponsorship, and advice that is designed specifically for each contract. Each agrees to an exchange in what both parties consider to be a fair trade. The partners must be explicit, describing clearly what they expect of each other and how they will know when they are living up to their ends of the partnership. The feedback they give each other will focus on being objective, positive, and specific. When critiquing the behavior or activities that seem counterproductive or off target, each must deliver the criticism as constructively and specifically as possible, focused on the behavior and not the person. Suggestions for improvement are requested, not given without solicitation. Each partner's goals and objectives are spelled out clearly and explicitly, so each knows what the other means. Then, each partner designs strategies or activities to achieve those goals with specific indicators to measure success: "how will I know when I'm there?" The goals are the "what" – the strategies are the "how."

Your Peer Mentor's role could take a number of forms. For example, she may be more politically savvy than you and might help you figure out which projects would get you the most visibility in your organization. She may help you understand how to influence your supervisor or others who have some say over your career and salary review. Similarly, your Peer Mentor could help you rehearse the talk you will have when you sit down with your boss. If you're in business or professional practice for yourself, your Peer Mentor could help you with your sales technique, financial planning, or advertising strategies. The Peer-Mentor model is based on the idea that the partners have an investment in and commitment to each other. There will undoubtedly be conflict, diversions, and distractions at times, but this is perfectly natural in an intimate and committed relationship.

In this book, I'll explain the concept of Peer Mentorship more fully and give a historical and anthropological overview of similar practices in various cultures through the ages. I'll explain how to find a Peer Mentor (or several) to achieve important goals in any category in your life. I'll show you ways to measure your success as the Peer Mentor relationship develops, how to select the best person for the contract, how to set realistic goals, how to create an actual Peer-Mentor Contract and how best to communicate with your partner. The book is organized on two levels: the first level is for the "I'm in a hurry to get started, cut to the chase, show me how" reader. For these readers, dive right in at Chapter 5 to get the description of the model, then immediately proceed onward to all the practical steps and exercises in Chapters 6 and beyond. For the other kind of reader who is also interested in learning about the societal and economic origins and roots of reciprocal processes before starting to implement these practices, then read Chapter 2, written by Dr Gabriella Djerrahian, an anthropologist at Université de Québec à Montréal, whose expertise and enthusiasm for the subject of reciprocity makes it a fascinating read. She has worked very hard to make some of these complex concepts very simple. The challenge, then, and the adventure, is to use these ideas, work through the obstacles, and achieve your goals towards success!

1.

THE DIFFERENCE THAT MAKES THE DIFFERENCE

Sometimes, what you're missing is <u>the</u> important ingredient for success!

There's a big problem in the world of career advancement today, especially among women. We are competent, educated, smart and ambitious yet somehow our big goals elude us.

The more advanced we are, the more difficult it becomes to admit that there are big gaps in our skills repertoire. When you're the division manager, it's hard to ask for help. This is even more true when you're a woman. The last thing you want is to seem like you're weak, and might need help in some areas.

So you "tough it out", "fake it till you make it", or whatever you tell yourself you have to do. But there's still something nagging at you. "If only I could understand how that system works". But who can I ask? I'm supposed to know this by now.

Imagine, though, that you had a "guardian angel" who could fill you in on the information you're missing, or don't understand, or wasn't included in your technical training for this job.

Wouldn't it be nice to know there was someone in your corner who was committed to helping you, who you trust, contributing to your success, without judging you or without ulterior motives?

Here are some lucky (and resourceful) women who found just that:

Kayamisha, a branding and marketing consultant to medium sized businesses landed a $ 400,000 project with a large publishing company. The work would take months and require several printed components.

Kayamisha had never managed such a large project. She would have to arrange for a letter of credit from the bank to pay the printers and other vendors. In the meantime, she was so preoccupied with getting this project done in time for the client's deadline that she was neglecting her other clients.

She had no idea how to manage the finances for something this complicated. Moreover, if any of the printed projects was not perfect, she would be responsible, having already paid the printers with the bank's line of credit, and have to re-do it at her expense.

A week earlier, at a networking meeting she had met a woman, Meredith, who was an accountant and financial advisor. Meredith had mentioned that she needed help with some sales materials for her practice.

Kayamisha contacted her, and they sat down and made a short-term agreement to help each other with their separate challenges . Kayamisha, confident she could trust Meredith having checked out her reputation and long standing relationships with loyal clients, got some good advice about managing her cash flow. Meredith got some tips on creating her sales brochures.

Gloria was an ophthalmologist who had graduated from her university program with honors, and had worked in the ophthalmology department of a major Canadian teaching hospital.

After several years, she decided to begin her own practice, sell beautiful eyewear and open a shop in her native Montreal. The only drawback was, she had no experience in retail store design or merchandising. Many of her existing patients followed her to her store for eye exams and to purchase new glasses.

But the shop didn't look very exciting or trendy; the window wasn't catchy-looking enough to attract the fashion-forward clientele she was seeking to buy high-end designer eyewear.

Joann, an interior designer, had just arrived in Montreal and was trying to get new clients there. But her French was rusty, and most of the wealthy French Canadian homeowners she wanted as clients required at least a modicum of French conversation to feel comfortable with the designer. Gloria was fluent in French; the two worked out a contract to help Gloria's store and window design,and to get Joann's "street French" up to speed for her new clientele.

Brenda had just been hired as the top legal counsel for Levi-Strauss, in San Francisco, one of the oldest clothing manufacturers in the country. Although the company had been around "forever" – they were one of the pioneers in many new forms of management – they embraced "ad hoc teams", "MBWA – Management by Walking Around" and the flat, rather than hierarchical organizational structure.

Brenda had come from a large, male-dominated law firm, and left because her goal of getting promoted to partner seemed unlikely.

What she found at her new post though, was her complete unfamiliarity with the style and norms of how the company functioned. She was used to the "top down" way of managing; when she held her first staff meeting, one after another the attorneys in her department asked questions, made suggestions and didn't at all wait for her to "lead" the meeting. They had been trained in the much more "democratic", participative style, which was the norm in the company.

Brenda realized she had to act fast. She approached Haley, an acquaintance who was a therapist (for groups and individuals) and asked her for coaching in "listening" and "facilitating" meetings. Of course she knew her desire for confidentiality in this relationship would be honored; as a licensed psychotherapist Haley would respect the therapist/client relationship.

What did Haley need? Legal advice to help her with a lawsuit in Small Claims Court (not really worth enough to hire counsel, but she still needed some basics to help her strategize her case).

Sandy, who had been working in the paint department of a big box home improvement store, had seen an increase in purchases of specialty paints, largely due to the improving construction market.

She decided to strike out on her own, and open a specialty paint store in her town. She knew all about the products, and was great at advising customers.

The challenge she was running into, though, was finding, screening and managing the mostly male employees and sub-contractors she would need. Painters are usually outside of the mainstream of the employment market, many are competent and responsible, but also some are ex-convicts, have substance abuse problems and other issues.

Sandy asked George, who owned a reputable moving company for advice on this matter. Movers have similar issues when hiring staff and contractors.

George was flattered to be considered an expert, and when he thought about it, he realized that Sandy had a skill that could help him. He asked her for suggestions on paint colors and brands to use to paint his moving trucks.

Their exchange of skills was not as formal as a Peer Mentor relationship, but Sandy was able to address the main "gap" in starting her new business.

As we shall see, there are many such examples of hurdles and challenges in businesses and careers, but now there can be a solution if you a) recognize what's missing and b) are resourceful in identifying someone who has what you need.

I hope that you will find the idea of a Peer Mentor intriguing, but more important, a practical and powerful way for you to achieve your goals!

2.

The Gift: Rituals of Exchange and Contract

Dr. Gabriella Djerrahian

Every year during the holidays, Christmas rolls around with a mega-frenzied shopping spree. Before I go any further, let me just get the deed done. I admit it. I'm one of *them*, a middle-class shopper who spends ridiculous amounts of money to buy presents for other middle-class recipients who really don't need them. Yet, every year, I find myself running amok from one shopping mall to the next, trying to come up with original gift ideas that will somehow outdo or, at the very least, equal what I gave last year.

None of the awesome presents I buy, buy, buy are for me - at least not at first glance. Like other holiday shoppers, everything I purchase is, well, to be given away. Now, before we start patting ourselves on the back in approbation of our infinite generosity, let me remind you that by the time New Year's rolls in, my pile of give-away presents has been replaced by a new pile of gifts that others bought expressly for me. For one thing, the gifts we let go of come back to us through highly ritualized exchanges - gifting and counter-gifting - in the commercial hoopla we call Christmas. So why go through the trouble of just moving stuff around from one person to the next, year after year, in a never-ending cycle of reciprocity? The answer is quite simple: gifting is a ritual that consolidates bonds between friends and families. It makes us feel good to show people we love just how much we care. And, yeah, I feel like a five-year-old kid when I open my presents. It's just plain fun.

We tend to think of rituals as the exclusive purview of tribes or ancient societies, the clichéd image of Native American men sitting in a circle on the floor, decorative headgear and all, passing along a pipe and exchanging presents with their white counterparts. Gift giving as a form of ritual, however, is alive and kicking in our modern, urban lives, and Christmas is not the only time when we participate in it. A few years back, a dear friend of mine announced that she was getting married. In the same breath she forbade us, her besties, from throwing her a bridal shower. This request did not go so well with mom-in-law-to-be. What do you mean there won't be a bridal shower?, she quipped. "Throughout the years," mama explained, "I have attended and given gifts at so many bridal showers, it's your turn to receive now." Her reaction clearly demonstrates another aspect of gift-giving based on rights and obligations: the right to collect what is 'due' to the new family into which my friend was marrying and the obligation to fulfill the role of both the giver and the receiver. There is also the issue of honor wrapped up in this. Letting others return our gifts to mark an important rite of passage in a woman's life, as marriage has traditionally been, allows the giver the opportunity to honor kin the same way that we have honored others in the past.

The idea of obligation in the form of gift giving is seldom mentioned out loud in our society. Nobody advertises Christmas as an opportunity to "buy more so you can get more." How selfish would that be? These anecdotes, however, underline the circulation of gifts and the untold obligation to return (and, in the last example, to receive). This ensures the circulation of goods that go around as presents. Cultural norms are crucial for determining who gives, who receives, what the goods circulating are, and how and when exchanges take place. Why do we continue to invest so much time and energy to perpetuate the gift cycle?

This is one of the questions that inspired the brilliant French sociologist Marcel Mauss (1872-1950) who wrote about it in his seminal essay called "The Gift: The form and reason for exchange in archaic societies," published in 1925. Almost a century ago, Mauss showed that what the gift does – the function it serves – is far more important than the actual gift itself. What power resides in the object given, he asked, that causes its recipient to pay it back?[1] To answer that, he delved into historical cases of gift giving, solidarity, and social relations in ancient civilizations and tribal societies.[2] This isn't to say that Mauss' own society had no role in his intellectual trajectory; on the contrary, Mauss wrote about the gift because he was inspired by rapid changes unfolding around him in twentieth-century Europe. Social inequalities and economic crises were increasing, and the push towards individualism in the wake of mass industrialization propelled him to think about the role of solidarity in emerging political and economic systems.

---

[1] P. 4, English translation of his book *The Gift: The Form and Reason for Exchange in Archaic Societies* (1923).

[2] Particularly from Polynesia, Melanesia and the North-West of Canada and the United States, and in various civilizations (Scandinavian, Babylonian, Roman, Germanic and Indian).

THE POTLATCH: A "TOTAL SERVICE"

Of the various gift-giving practices that Mauss described, the *potlatch* captured the imagination of generations of readers and came to epitomize the essence of his book. The potlatch is a complex gift giving ceremony institutionalized by some Native American communities along the Canadian and American North-West Pacific Coast. While varieties existed in the way that potlatches were structured, Mauss drew from the general idea of the potlatch and highlighted a common feature: the competitive gifting and counter-gifting ceremonial feasts that occurred within the framework of hospitality and rivalry. In extreme cases rivalry between opposing tribes led to combat, violence and even death. Let's call this more dramatic category of potlatches "extreme gift-giving."

For Mauss, the potlatch is nothing more than a system of gifts exchanged, or, as he called it, a "gift economy." To put it simply, a chief would throw a huge party for a bunch of tribes. The objective of the ceremony would be for him to show off his high social standing by giving away his wealth (gifting) in a way that competed with the guests' ability to do the same towards the host (counter-gifting). The word potlatch itself has been translated into "giving" (in Chinook), or "to give" (from the Nootka verb "pa-chide").[3] In some cases, showing off not only meant redistributing one's wealth according to the donor's assessment of the receiver's worth, but its sheer destruction as well. The elites' title of chief was put to the test based on how much they were able to get rid of by gifting or destroying, following a period of accumulation for the purpose of potlatching.

Not all potlatches were of this combative – or agonistic to use Mauss' term – nature. Moreover, it wasn't only about huffing, puffing and oversized male egos. People feasted, gifts circulated,

---

[3] Risdale, Frank. 1997. A Discussion of the Potlatch and Social Structure, TOTEM : The University of Western Ontario Journal of Anthropology, Vol. 3, Issue 2, article 3.

and alliances were made and broken. Titles and, accordingly, social hierarchies were re-assigned. Outdoing one another through the act of giving away wealth was orchestrated by rituals that took place within a highly complex legal and political system.

Mauss used information gathered by other scholars to put together his analysis of the potlatch. He consulted documents written by people who witnessed first-hand how the tribes mentioned in *The Gift* used to live. These accounts were largely collected from the late 1800s to the early 1900s when colonial interference and European domination over native populations started to bear important changes in the potlatch. *The Gift* was written at a time of massive transformation and cultural loss for these communities. For Canadian authorities, the potlatch represented one of the most important obstacles to killing off native cultures and "taking the Indian out of the Indian."[4] In their quest to "civilize" Canada's indigenous population, the government banned the potlatch between 1884 and 1951, making it a legal offence. The destruction of valuable objects like copper only reinforced their objective to kill off the potlatch once and for all. Authorities could not wrap their heads around the act of deliberately getting rid of one's own material wealth through its annihilation. It countered the very idea of the capitalist society Euro-Americans were so keen on building. In our society, one attains success and fortune through the accumulation, and not the distribution, of wealth. The potlatch represents the polar opposite. Now, for those of us too eager to evoke the tired, romantic idea of the altruistic and selfless "noble savage" who is really about peace and sharing, Mauss offered a powerful antidote. The purpose, it seems, of giving away wealth was to gain more in the form of honor, power, and prestige. Once again, Mauss showed that gift giving is really a system of exchange and that gifting is not a random act of kindness, even in the case of the potlatch.

---

[4] Grinde 2004.

The potlatch touched upon every aspect of life in the communities where it took place. For this reason, Mauss considered it a "total service."[5] The concept of total service also alludes to the fact that the chief was the combative mediator who gifted and counter-gifted his clans' wealth on behalf of the collective as a whole. Through his study of the potlatch, Mauss argued for a more holistic, or "total," approach to the gift because the potlatch represented a religious, spiritual, economic, juridical, and social affair that mobilized all aspects of a community. Though the act of gift giving is conducted by an individual giver to an individual receiver, person-to-person gift exchanges take their symbolic cues from the collective framework of relationships between groups. In the context of the potlatch, gifts were not anonymous objects but rather, had their own spirit imbued with the identity of the giver and of the larger group to which they belonged.

THE KULA RING

Mauss spent an important part of the book introducing another gift exchange circle found among natives of the Trobriand Islands called the *kula* in what is today Papua New Guinea. His analysis is based on information he gathered from anthropologist Branislow Malinowski, who spent years doing observations in the region starting from 1914. Malinowski was stuck there due to the outbreak of World War I and could not return to Europe. He spent hours observing the kula, among other practices. The kula ring refers to a large exchange network in which goods moved between islands and communities. The two most valuable trade commodities were armshells and necklaces, which circulated in different directions. Whereas armshells moved counter-clockwise, necklaces were traded in the opposite direction.

---

[5] See p. 7 of the English translation of *The Gift: The Form and Reason for Exchange in Archaic Societies* (1923) for an explanation.

Malinowski wondered why people would go to so much trouble, at times navigating dangerous waters from island to island, in order to maintain a circle of exchange of non-utilitarian goods. The observations he reported about the kula clearly demonstrated that the natives of the Islands were indeed capable of rational thinking. Attributing the capacity of rational thinking to the Islanders went against the general notion of the day that equated 'savages' to 'backwardness' and a lack of intelligence. Instead, Malinowski argued that the kula is a highly complex gift economy that is really about political authority. Items traded did not have a utilitarian use but they had social, political and spiritual value. Both armshells and necklaces represented social status and were part of a much larger system of exchange that included useful goods such as food, hospitality and in some cases, women. Mauss considered the kula to be the extreme example of a larger, more general network of exchange within and between tribes.

Once again, as with the potlatch, Mauss applied the principle of the kula to unveil the idea of a contract in regards to gift giving. The contract of the gift goes against our general assumption that gift giving is a voluntary act divorced from interest, reciprocity and expectations. The examples of the kula and the potlatch show us that what appears to be at first glance gift giving in its purest form, in other words without strings attached, is actually linked to interests and obligations that regulate spiritual life, economy, kinship and political alliances between giver and receiver.

Like Malinowski who applied the example of the kula to demonstrate that natives were actually rational-thinking beings, Mauss' study of the gift offered a commentary on the capitalist ideology of wealth through accumulation by presenting both the potlatch and the kula as an alternative to the capitalist market. In western societies we consider that more, more, more translates into wealth and success. For native communities who practiced the potlatch, wealth was translated into the value and prestige of what one gave away or expedited through destruction. Doing so was a direct reflection of the value and prestige of the giver's worth and social standing. Contrary to the logic of the capitalist market, the goods exchanged within the gift economy were not about maximizing economic and material profit.

In eighteenth- and nineteenth century European thought, the native had been revered as a 'noble savage' not yet polluted by the obligations of a modern life. Whatever romanticized notion of the 'noble savage' as altruistic and selfless beings that Rousseau and others portrayed evaporated with Malinowski and Mauss' works, among others. Keeping tabs, being selfish, and wanting more (more wealth to keep as possessions or more wealth to give away and get more prestige) were just as alive and well in "tribal" communities of the past as they are in our own society. What then, is the difference between exchanges of goods as commodity and exchanges of goods as gifts?

GIFT AND COMMODITY EXCHANGE[6]

Economists and social scientists have long thought about what constitutes a transaction of goods and services between two parties. What makes an exchange commercial in nature? How are economic transactions different from the exchange of gifts and counter-gifts? Let me begin by giving a play-by-play of some of the key ideas that economists and other scholars have considered in thinking about the difference between commodity- and gift-exchange.

According to Mauss, there is a difference to be made between gift exchange, as described in the examples of the potlatch and the kula, and commodity exchange. He believed that the economy of small-scale societies such as the Trobriand Islanders and Native American communities like the Kwakiutl revolved around gift exchanges. At the heart of the distinction between both types of systems is the quality of social relations. In the gift exchange,

---

[6] This section is based on an article published by Andrej Rus in 2008: "'Gift vs. commodity' debate revisited," *Anthropological Notebooks*, 14 (1), pp. 81-102.

people are reciprocally bound even after the transaction is complete, and there is a high level of interdependency between both parties. The receiver continually holds an obligation to the giver and vice versa, leading to a circular flow of exchanges that insures the maintenance of long-term relationships. What determines the value of goods exchanged is not their economic value, but rather their social, spiritual, political, and symbolic worth. In these communities, the gift forges alliances, bringing people together in a dance of giving and receiving, giving and receiving, giving and receiving. Essentially, the function of the exchange was to uphold a moral purpose. Moreover, the goods being gifted were thought to be imbued with life. Gifts carry their own spirit from owner to owner.

In commodity exchanges, the basis of capitalist societies, the transaction occurs between two parties, often strangers to one another, who engage in trade or barter. Social relation is not a precursor to the transaction, nor is it necessarily something that the transaction gives rise to. The obligation to return and the moral concerns prevalent in gift exchanges are not primary considerations. Economic value of the commodity prevails in all other aspects, and it lacks in "symbolic uniqueness." The idea of profit and economic rationality are central tenets of commodity exchange. This, of course, is not to say that gift giving ceremonies like the potlatch and the kula did not abide by their own economic and calculated logic of exchange, but that the purpose and the means of those exchanges varied significantly from commodity exchanges, among other differences. As we saw in the example of the potlatch and the kula, self- and collective-interests are guiding principles in gift exchanges. Others point out that the main difference between gift exchange and simple barter is the lapse of time between the act of giving and counter-giving.[7]

What is interesting in terms of peer-to-peer mentoring is that exchanges in the form of gift giving are not so different from trade

---

[7] Pp 84, Rus 2008.

or barter in that rationality, self-interest and economy characterize both transaction types. Exchange is really about reciprocity, whether the cycle of gifting and counter-gifting comes full circle on the spot (during Christmas, for example) or at a later time and place (during birthdays and other occasions).

Let's bring back the potlatch ban for a minute. It's quite safe to say that the practice of destroying valuable goods, particularly copper, goes against every fiber of our hyper-consumer ethos. If we take a closer look at our own Christmas gifting carnival, it's not hard to see how the expenditure of thousands upon thousands of dollars each year is, well, kind of silly. I'm not bringing up this point to suggest that we should stop gifting or showing appreciation to those we love by way of presents. What I am pointing to, however, is that the way we do this is through commercialism, and that this is very much a symptom of the consumption-based societies we live in. Of course, there are alternatives to status quo gifting practices, yet none of them have gone mainstream. For one, we could make our own gifts, but then again, who in their right mind would do that? Imagine having to make gifts every time your child had a birthday party! Just the thought is enough to make a working mom go crazy. Another option would be to re-gift, lest we be labeled a "re-gifter" like in the Seinfeld episode in which Jerry received a label maker from the dentist Tim Whately, only to discover that Elaine had originally given Tim that same gift. Tim's outing as a re-gifter who recycled the label maker was anything but a compliment.

One of the more important concepts we can take away from Mauss' *The Gift* is that pure gifts do not really exist, whether in small non-Western communities or in large-scale Western societies. Systems of exchanges, be they gift- or commodity-exchanges, share many characteristics (economic calculation, self interest, obligation to return, etc.) and are based on a common principle: entering a contract. A contract binds two parties to an exchange in which details have been thought out and agreed upon prior to accepting the agreement. Implicit contracts are the basis of our economic functioning. When I happily overpay for a cup of frappa-mocha-slightly-warmed-up-lattucino-with-non-soya-soya-milk, I hand over my money to the cashier fully trusting that he or she will deliver, whatever hilarity might ensue about the fluffed up names we now use instead of "coffee."

These contracts are verbal, while others are written and/or legally binding. The peer-to-peer mentorship contract discussed by Elaina in this book is a great example of non-monetary transactions. I suspect that Mauss would gladly re-think some aspects of his book in light of the way goods and services are being exchanged today.

PEER-TO-PEER ECONOMY: "WHY BUY WHEN YOU CAN BORROW"?

The collaborative economy, as the sharing economy is also called, is booming in Canada and the United States. There is a movement of regular citizens who are doing away with possessiveness and making accessible what they own. Cars, homes, beds, sofas, home appliances, clothes, lifts, bicycles, and even internet connectivity, solar power, working stations, and money are some examples of peer-to-peer services that can be exchanged or rented out. Combined with technological advances and the hyper-connectivity afforded by the Internet, peer-to-peer service companies are thriving, whether transactions are non-monetary as in trade or barter, or monetary transactions. On this platform of sharing, ownership is taking second seat to access as start-up companies the world over are tapping into the sheer financial profit generated at the crossroads of collaboration, exchange, and the market.

Peer-to-peer service companies offer commodity exchanges between two strangers entering a contract agreement. There is no previous social relationship between giver and receiver, and once the transaction is completed, both parties part ways without strings attached. No other obligations bind them together except for what the implicit exchange contract called for. The networks established through the collaborative economy, in other words connections between people, facilitated through the platform of exchange offered by technology, put a dent in Mauss' division. For one, peer-to-peer sharing engages a higher level of trust between two strangers compared to other commercial transactions. It's one thing for me to go to a store and buy a pint of milk, trusting that the cashier will let me leave with the bottle once I hand over the money; it's another thing entirely to lead a complete stranger to my cow. More than ever before we are making goods and services that are part of our intimate worlds available for consumption by complete strangers. Trust, therefore, has taken center-stage in collaborative economic transactions. Online reviews also play a crucial role in keeping potential clients on track. We are opening our doors and putting up for rent elements of our inner spheres – our couches, our homes, our beds – in ways that have seriously challenged conventional norms of commerce.

These emerging practices of the shared economy, as it is often called, are not as smooth as some enthusiasts would have us believe. This is obvious when looking at the uproar that Uber has created. Taxi drivers are up in arms as the popularity of the transportation service continues to boom, and there are other concerns to be addressed in terms of safety, insurance, legal responsibility in case of accidents, etc as well. While these details are being worked out from location to location, Uber is going strong. But, exactly how "shared" can a service like Uber be on a global scale? I'm more interested in looking at those of us – by and large most of the world – who are at the margins of the shared economy, those on the outside looking in. Renting out your bed, your car, and your home requires that you possess them. Sure, it is much cheaper – not to mention a completely different kind of travel experience – to couch surf in Thailand and meet local Thais your age savvy enough to be connected to the Internet and make use of it for their economic advantage, instead of renting a lonely hotel room or a bed in a hostel. But questioning who gets to participate in this new commodity exchange is enough to realize that the shared economy is not that shared after all.

While it works for many, as the growing popularity of the shared services proves, in many other cases it reinforces some of the staggering economic inequalities already in place.

The great thing about peer mentoring is that it does not necessarily require money, since the currency is skill. Another important element for peer mentoring to be put in practice is communication. Communication is the means for making our skills aware to a group of peers so that we can match skill or service offers with skill or service needs. Think of Peer-mentoring as networking taken to a whole new level. Networking in the framework of peer-mentoring is like networking squared, so to speak, because it involves more than accumulating professional contacts: it requires establishing a socially meaningful, reciprocal and interactive system of exchange between two parties who enter a work contract. In many ways, it is our modern version of gift giving, a new twist to the older systems of exchanges that Mauss and Malinowski talk about.

3.

The Sharing Economy: Making a Living, One Gig at a Time

Thinking about Peer Mentoring made me realize how many changes are taking place in our society. These changes are caused partly by the current recession and partly by the growing awareness that we all have uncultivated resources—unused talents and skills—that we could share with others, if we chose. First, though, we have to do two things: identify specifically what those resources are and find people to share them with. Today's economy seems ripe for this Peer-Mentoring model to take hold, as people are now accustomed to the idea of sharing resources of all kinds. Many of us already offer our bedrooms, couches, cars, or *office* spaces to others for their use. From there, it's not a distant leap to sharing our personal resources with others—our skills, know-how, and contacts—and receiving their resources in return.

The examples I'll use in this chapter are mostly about sharing material resources. I visualize this happening within the framework of a large-scale system—a central registry of customers—that manages and facilitates circulation among members. A library is the perfect example. As we'll see later, though, the more personal kind of Peer Mentoring is very different. It consists of directly sharing personal resources with one specific person—in the context of a contract, and with no money exchanged. In this situation, no central company or registry is involved. First, let's look at sharing practices that occur in organized and regulated structures like libraries.

OLDIES BUT GOODIES: CENTRALIZED EXCHANGES IN ACTION

As soon as I finish writing this section, I'll head across the street to my local library (Westmount Library, a 100-year-old architectural landmark in beautiful Montreal, where I live), which offers one of the oldest, most common and trusted forms of 'peer-sharing'. This branch also has a small section for recycled (used) books, which have been donated by neighbors and sold as "books for a buck." I booked a private conference room to meet with Gabriella, the anthropologist who wrote the previous chapter. This service (allowing members to use a meeting space) is another shared resource offered by the library. On the way to the library, I'll pass the BIXI bike stand, which is a citywide bike sharing service. You can pick up a bike at this location, use it for a few hours, and then drop it at another stand, way across town.

I will be picking up a car from the parking lot outside the library, which belongs to Communauto, a Canadian car-sharing service similar to Zip-Car. As a member, I've made a reservation online. Then, I'll use my members' key to unlock a lockbox on a tree in the parking lot, remove the key for the car I've booked, and off I'll go. Four hours later, I'll bring the car back to this lot, log the number of kilometers I've driven, and return to my home. I won't have a bill for parking, insurance, or gas. I can do this as many times a month as I want. I pay an annual fee, plus a usage fee for the hours I've had the vehicle and the number of kilometers I've driven. Now Communauto has instituted a new service called "peer-sharing." Local car owners can get their vehicles checked out by mechanics, to make sure they're sound, and then offer them to be used by Communauto members. The car owner gets paid a rental fee for this and Communauto can now offer more options to its members.

Until recently, I didn't have a word for it, but I now know that I am a member of what is being called 'the sharing economy.' This is an intricate network of buyers and sellers or groups of people who partake of a single resource such as the use of compact cars or bicycles in large cities. This has come about with the confluence of two forces. The first is technology: inexpensive computing power allows a freelance artist to create a company's brochure that can rival the services of a much larger promotion agency at a fraction of the cost. In fact, that freelancer might have been the Art Director of such an agency who was laid off and is working now as an independent contractor. The second force is new social habits. We hear a lot about the "99%" and the "1%," the growing income disparity in our society. As the gap between the "haves" and the "have-nots" widens, we now have people who have money, but no time, and people who have time but no money.

Getting back to the realm of transportation, there are many variations on the idea of several people sharing a single resource. Communauto has just instituted a service of point-to-point vehicle use called "cars-2-go." New to many U.S. cities are Lyft and Uber. I recently heard of a young man who had lived in New York all his life, wanted to leave, but didn't know how to drive and had a fear of freeway systems. He moved to L.A., joined Uber, and has a car pick him up and take him to his destination by using an app on his smartphone. As a response to many people raising concerns about the safety of women being driven in Uber cars by men who are not official employees with mandatory ID's, a new niche has been created. It is a variation of Uber that has started in New York City called She-Taxi and it now employs 300 female drivers who will chauffeur an exclusively female group of customers. As the well-known economist Tom Friedman wrote in the New York Times recently, "the sharing economy is alive and well, and it's thriving in many sectors of the economy and geographic areas."

In addition to personal benefits, it's become terribly cool to be part of the sharing economy. As recently as six or seven years ago, it might have been a source of deep embarrassment and shame for someone of my age and socioeconomic status to be seen driving a Communauto rental vehicle with a prominent logo consisting of concentric green circles on both front doors. I would have considered it much higher status to be sporting a BMW or Mercedes, gas-guzzling be damned. Now I, and many of my friends, feel it's vulgar and ecologically tone-deaf to be driving a large vehicle. Think of your reaction the last time you tried to park next to a Hummer. During the same several hours of any day, in any city or town, hundreds of thousands of ordinary people are making use of these shared services. For some, sharing for profit is a natural instinct and is nurtured from an early age. Zhang Lei, a billionaire investor in Internet companies, got his start with a sharing economy when, at age 7, he rented his comic books to commuters waiting for trains at the local commuter station.

In other types of peer-sharing, for example Task Rabbit, people who are unemployed or underemployed become "micro-entrepreneurs" by offering skills they have on a network that is organized by areas of skill and geographically. Even geography need not be a barrier for many tasks anymore. Not long ago, I needed someone to help me organize my thoughts and then word-process a chart I had created for this book and for some seminars I was planning to give. I went on TaskRabbit and found a young woman, a stay-at-home mom who had worked as an executive assistant, located in California. We discussed the project via email and agreed on a price and due date. She delivered a beautiful job on time; I paid TaskRabbit via Paypal, and it paid her the agreed-upon amount minus the share TaskRabbit takes.

My niece, who is a busy single rabbi in a small town near Boston, was pregnant and wanted to hire a nanny as soon as the baby was born. She hired a "screener" (who happened to be in Chicago) to interview nannies and give her a list of the five best candidates in the Boston area. The process took a few weeks; then she interviewed the finalists via Skype and hired one, who has worked out wonderfully. She saved herself hours of scrolling through ads and resumes, and since this was her first child, she wanted an expert to help her form a list of criteria and then interview prospects. She paid TaskRabbit for that service. She also wrote a short review of her experience. This review process is a very important aspect of most peer-sharing services; we will return to this topic shortly.

I have used a similar service called fiverr. It is a resource upon which people list gigs they will perform and name a fee (e.g. "I will transcribe your audio for $25"). Members purchase gigs and then communicate with their supplier through fiverr's website. It is quite restrictive regarding the buyer and seller's direct communication in an effort to prevent people from meeting on the site then working together outside of the website in an attempt to avoid paying its fees, If, in a message you send to your seller, you mention a word like "money," "pay," or "compensation," a red message pops up reminding you that you may not go around the website and hire the supplier directly. That aside, I have had some tasks done very well and delivered on time by this service.

Here are some other examples of peer sharing, some of which I've practiced informally for years. Several years ago, when I lived on the Upper East Side of New York City and was working in Northern New Jersey, I purchased a very inexpensive car with a partner, who lived on the Upper West Side and was a professor at a university in Brooklyn. If you know the geography of New York, you'll know how much of a hardship reverse commuting would have been for each of us without a car. Also, the cost of a full-time parking space in either of our neighborhoods would have been prohibitive. So, we shared. He would go to his job, return to Manhattan, and leave me a phone message telling me where he had parked the car (and when it had to be moved – parking laws in New York are very strictly enforced, and you can find your vehicle towed if you overstay your street parking space by even a few minutes). This arrangement lasted for a few years and, in the process, we became great friends. Later, when he and his wife moved to Israel, they even offered me their Jerusalem guest room for a few weeks.

After this successful sharing, I bought another car and shared it with another friend, a jazz musician who was home during the daytime hours and could move the car from one parking spot to another when I was at my corporate office. In return, he got the car most weekends.

A lot of sharing practices begin informally, word spreads and they become entrenched in their unique practices. In the early 90's in New York's Upper East Side, people heading to work on Wall Street took the long subway ride or shared taxis. I don't know how it started, but every morning from 6 to about 8:30am, long lines formed at the corner of York Avenue and 79th Street. Cabs would pull up, fill up with four or five passengers, speed on towards the FDR drive, and head non-stop to a certain corner on Wall Street. The fare was $10 per person, paid directly to the cabbie (which included a tip). Most of the commuters didn't know each other and certainly didn't talk during the ride. Everyone read his or her newspaper, and eating or chatting was not permitted. Break one of these implicit rules and you ran the risk of being banned from the line. I think there was a return trip option, but since I didn't work near Wall Street, I'm unsure.

Another category that is now part of the sharing economy is travel (business or leisure). Airbnb, which is now a huge network, started when a few young Silicon Valley roommates were asked quite unexpectedly to host a few visiting businesspeople from Asia because all the hotels were booked. They had no guest room, so they inflated a few air mattresses and gave their guests a reasonably comfortable (and free) stay. The next time this happened, they didn't refuse their guests' offer to pay. Soon, they were running an ad-hoc bed and breakfast and other friends were renting out their spare rooms, or entire apartments, for short periods. All the guests and hosts were listed on the group's website, which matched up available accommodations with guests who needed them. Payments were made through the site, which deducted a handling fee or commission from the payment amount.

airbnb is a now a worldwide operation that boasts 800,000 listings in more than 34,000 locations. It provides an extra income stream for ordinary people to help pay their rent or mortgage, reasonably priced lodgings for travellers, and a more personal and casual relationship between guest and host. In some cases, guests become hosts when their former hosts visit *them*.

In New York, many years ago, a company called Feathered Nest allowed New York residents to rent out their apartments or extra rooms (hardly anyone in New York City has an extra room) to customers from out of town. This was largely under the radar, however, because landlords frowned upon this sort of activity. I once rented out my rent-controlled apartment for short periods while I travelled extensively for business. My landlord (we called him "Mr. So Sue Me") found out and wasn't happy. I was treading on the thin gray line of legality so I stopped doing it, although the extra money was great. But a rent-controlled apartment is too precious a commodity in New York to risk losing.

Today, in fact, there is again a dispute between the Rental Board of New York and airbnb, with the board claiming that tenants don't have the right to, in effect, operate a bed and breakfast or hospitality service without a proper commercial license. Still, airbnb is different from past services, since it is all online and provides great choices in many locations for ordinary travellers. Its quality control system is also online; guests are encouraged to write reviews after their stays. A good review gives a host a few gold stars and of course enhances her reputation. Accordingly, any complaints mar a host's standing. The site publishes them all, without censoring, so customers can judge for themselves.

I CAN GET IT FOR YOU WHOLESALE

The consignment or resale shop has been around for ages, but now it has gone mainstream and upscale. Now there are some online versions of consignment shopping. Two sites I know, Tradesy and Poshmark, allow customers from all over the U.S. to "consign." This is done virtually; they post photos and information about the items for sale. These include designer clothing, shoes, bags, jewelry, and accessories. When a customer makes a purchase, the consigner ships directly from her home, and is paid the agreed-upon price minus a commission for the middle-man, the website. The site makes money, does not need a bricks-and-mortar store, and all customers and sellers are happy.

A wealthy, petite friend of mine, who goes to many social events in the city (and can't be seen in the same outfit twice) invites her other petite socialite friends to a "clothing swap" once a year. The ladies have wine and snacks and go home with "gently worn" designer outfits for the next party season.

PROFESSIONAL SHARING

We also see sharing practices in professional services and advice. I belong to a group called SNN, Speaker News Network, a virtual network of about 8,000 professional speakers and trainers. We are emailed a newsletter every week, as well as several educational offerings in the form of webinars, teleseminars, and advice.

SNN has come up with a wonderful, creative way of getting a steady stream of good content for the newsletter. We don't pay a membership fee to receive the newsletter. Instead, we are asked to submit two "tips" every quarter to be shared with the entire membership. These can be ideas we have created, better ways to speak and train, websites we've discovered that have helpful information, and even ideas on business travel. This is truly an example of peers helping peers, and, because of the rules, I'm always thinking of ways I can offer a tip or idea to my fellow consultants and speakers.

Many years ago, in New York City, I belonged to a Writers' Support Group. Rather than being overly easygoing at these meetings and merely talking about writer's block and annoying publishers, we followed a strictly disciplined regimen. We met once a week at someone's apartment and we had a group facilitator (a different one each time) who ran the process. Each person was "on" for the whole weekly session; he or she would have prepared a chapter (or a chunk) of work to read to the group and distribute a neatly typed copy to each member. The facilitator would allow time for the reading, then go around the group to answer questions like: Best line, Worst line, What I learned, What I wish I would have learned, What to edit out, Suggestions for improvement, etc. The person in the hot seat had to just listen; someone took notes of all the comments and ideas for him or her to take home and absorb. Then we'd all have coffee and dessert and a few laughs—and <u>not</u> talk about writing

We were all writing different genres of work: we had a murder mystery novelist, a poet, a self-help author, a business writer (me), a romance novelist, a screenwriter, a playwright, and even a PR person. But we all got the help we needed, and we were enriched by exposure to other kinds of writing, as well as different perspectives from the other members.

Another example of business and professional peer sharing is LinkedIn, which is a vast international network of contacts. As of this writing, there are 332 million members in 200 countries, plus thousands of like-minded subgroups, where people can discuss issues of common interest. Unlike Facebook, Twitter, Pinterest, or Instagram, LinkedIn is all about business and professional networking. In my own business, I have found and formed, via LinkedIn, productive mutual relationships with affiliates in India, the Philippines, and all over the U.S.. I even visited India last year and was graciously hosted by my affiliate there. He organized a seminar for 25 of his executive clients; I taught it, and we followed up together for future business. I would <u>never</u> have found this talented professional or benefited from business connections made in New Delhi without LinkedIn.

In the realm of real estate, this time in commercial or office space, small business owners often join up to share a space. In the 90s, when Silicon Valley in California was home to hundreds of start-ups, some of which couldn't or wouldn't work in people's basements any longer, some smart real estate developers began what were called incubators. A business owner would rent a small space and share common services like secretaries, clerical help, and even photocopy machines and computers. Not only was this a great savings financially for the participants, it also provided an environment for peers to discuss theories, bounce ideas off each other, and share contacts or other resources.

When I started my business in New York City, I fell in love with a 4,000 square foot space in the "Flatiron" district. It was not yet the hip area it is now (some call it Silicon Alley). Still, the rents were astronomical, as they always have been in the city. And the address was on Madison Avenue. I HAD to have it! But there was no way I could afford it on my own. I placed an ad in a few local business magazines and journals and ended up with entrepreneurs sharing my space. We hired a secretary, shared a conference room/library, and helped each other with client problems and business challenges. We became great and trusted friends, often ordered lunch from the deli downstairs and ate together in our conference room, sharing that day's business challenges and triumphs, and, most importantly, offering fresh perspectives to each other. The element of sociability is an important benefit in this arrangement

Our businesses were vastly different from one another: Michael ran a small ad agency, Richard helped doctoral students with their research, Albert did corporate and industrial design, I was running a training and consulting business, and Rosemary also did consulting, but it was quite different from mine. What we had in common was a desire to succeed, a need to save money, a place of business where we could invite clients (as opposed to working at home in our apartments), a preference for professional companionship, and last but not least, a desire for a highly coveted Madison Avenue address. Every year we hosted an "orphans' office Holiday Party" for people who were independent entrepreneurs like ourselves and so didn't have an office party to go to.

Now, many companies rent office space to professionals or small business owners. In New York, there is a company called "LawFirm Suites" which rents spaces to attorneys for short- and long-term stays. It advertises that its offices are "designed by lawyers for lawyers". I'm not sure what actual designers would have to say, but it seems to work very well for their clients. One can rent a conference room for a day to host a meeting or a cubicle for a few months. Others, like ShareDesk, offer short-term rentals—a desk, an office, and a menu of many office services. It has partnered with more than 2,400 venues in 440 cities across 70 countries and is still growing. Such firms are capitalizing on several converging trends: increased costs of commercial real estate, which make it prohibitive for many professionals to rent full-time office space; increased travel and business across state lines and internationally, offering professionals "an office in every city"; and the economic benefits of using clerical and other office services on an as-needed basis.

As we can see from all these examples, sharing is definitely the zeitgeist of the moment. As large companies downsize, more and more people are finding themselves (or choosing to be) in the "gig" economy. And while it has worked well for many people, releasing them from the restraints of a 9 to 5 life, there still is a need for human contact, support and motivation. This is a perfect opportunity for creating a Peer Mentor partnership, a helpful "kick in the can'ts."

Resources

1. Article by Jeremiah Owyang on the categories and types of Collaborative Economy markets:

   - http://www.web-strategist.com/blog/2013/02/24/the-master-list-of-the-collaborative-economy-rent-and-trade-everything/

2. This is a comprehensive list, by category, of all the sharing services currently available in the U.S. and worldwide (as of May 2015) No doubt by the time you read this, the list will have expanded.

   - http://www.collaborativeconsumption.com/

4.

Barter: How many Cows for That Smartphone?

When I began gathering information and my thoughts for writing this book, the idea of barter came to my mind. As we'll see when we explore the main concept of Peer Mentoring, the fundamental exchange that the two people are engaging in is a barter of their separate, not necessarily equal, but equivalent resources, skills, and gifts. Barter, as a form of exchange is not a new concept. In fact, there are numerous historical situations in which it was the method *par excellence*. Much like Peer Mentoring, different yet equivalent goods and services were swapped between two parties. How such goods and services were evaluated and who held the authority to define their value changed over time. In this next section, I introduce a few examples, many of which I draw from the work of historians, where two people or parties entered an exchange contract and engaged in barter.[8]

---

[8] Many of the historical facts about barter described here are condensed from the the Overview in Chapter 1 of *The Complete Idiot's Guide to Barter & Trade Exchanges* by Jerry Howell and Tom Chmielewski (2009 Penguin Group).

A BRIEF OVERVIEW OF BARTER

The colonial era in America was primarily a barter economy. Goods included beaver pelts, corn, nails, tobacco, and deerskins. Actually, buckskin trading gave us our modern slang for dollar, "buck." After the American Revolution, the United States began to print paper money, but inflation was so bad that people turned to barter again. It is to be noted that whenever the economy is in poor condition, barter booms. When the Crash of 1929 was followed by the Great Depression, large numbers of people lost their jobs and cash was scarce as a result. These people still had goods and skills, so they began trading what goods, services, and resources they could offer for food, lodging, or whatever they needed. In 1931, a group of labor activists formed the UCL (Unemployed Citizens League) of Seattle. By 1933, the UCL had created a barter economy for its 200,000 members. Other organizations soon followed, taking the barter concept further. They issued "scrip," substitute money, representing an IOU redeemable at multiple businesses or exchanges. As the economy stabilized, some of the barter organizations faded, but the gas crisis of the 1970's and the recession in the early 1980's led to another rise in barter clubs.

Another dimension also appeared in the form of commercial trade exchanges and brokering business-to-business deals through indirect barter. When international companies use this concept, it is called "countertrade," linking imports and exports in a trade transaction that takes place without money.

BARTER AND EARLY CURRENCIES

Barter is almost as old as civilization. Academics trace its beginnings to around 9000 BC when cattle was first domesticated and considered a tangible asset. People could trade some of their herd (sheep, cows, or camels) for other things, which their family needed: food, water, a spear, or a shield. Believed to be first discovered in Egypt and depicted on the walls of tombs, cowrie shells were used by the Chinese in approximately 1200 BC as a form of currency. By some, they were even considered to hold magic powers. The Chinese were so taken by cowrie shells that they began to copy their shapes in base metals.

In parts of the Middle East, pieces of metal, small enough to carry around, became a more practical currency. Egyptians used lumps of gold in the shape of small sheep because sheep were the basis for their trading. Lydia, a part of what is now Turkey, circulated a bean-shaped coin made of a mix of gold and silver in around 600 BCE. They added a stamped design to their "coins" to attest to their standard weight and value. With that change, lumps of metal no longer had to be weighed to determine their worth. The images of the stamps were of the rulers and of various gods. This form of coin began showing up in Greek, Persian, Macedonian, and Roman empires. Unlike the Chinese coins made from base metals, the new coins were made from scarce, precious metals such as bronze, gold, and silver.

It was the Chinese, in around the ninth century C.E. (the Sung dynasty), who issued the first paper money, at first to offset a shortage of copper. It seemed like a good idea at the time, until the government printed unlimited paper money, causing hyperinflation. By 1455, paper money had become worthless and the new Ming dynasty banned it for hundreds of years. The first bank note in China was not paper, but leather. Historians say that in 1180 BCE bank notes were 1-foot squares of white deerskin, with edges in vivid colors. It wasn't until 1661 CE that the first issue of paper money began in Europe – the Stockholm Bank introduced the first banknotes, but they circulated too many and had to call in the government to help. Sound familiar?

As Europeans came to the Americas, their interactions with Native Americans included barter and direct trades. European traders used beads and trinkets, also a lot of military items like guns and ammunition, and, most importantly, alcohol to trade for territory, food, clothes, and other resources. Native Americans gave strong cultural value and significance to shell beads – the word "wampum," still used as a slang meaning for "money," is a shortened version of the Algonquin word "wampumpeage" or "white shell beads." Wampum carried strong symbolic importance in religious, social, and political practices. Archaeologists have found similar materials and inferred their uses farther south and even on the California coast. When Jacques Cartier first travelled to what is now Canada, he reported that white shell beads were used by the St. Lawrence Iroquois in 1535. He compared those beads to the use of gold and silver as money among the Europeans. By the seventeenth century, wampum became a kind of currency between settlers and Native Americans. The website, nativetech.org quotes a report of the eighteenth century that "a fathom (6 feet) of strung beads of white wampum was worth 10 shillings and double that for purple beads," which shows that English settlers in the colonies used wampum (learned from the people they colonized) as their own coinage.

Over the next several hundred years, barter practices continued in some form or another, particularly during tough economic times, when cash was scarce, but people still needed goods and services.

BARTER IN THE TWENTY-FIRST CENTURY

The 2008 recession has renewed interest in barter, for individuals and for businesses. In direct barter, the biggest challenge was finding someone who wanted what you had and had what you needed. But now the Internet allows you to search the world for the match you want. The "Barter" section on Craigslist exploded in 2008 and 2009 – transactions can be as simple as one family offering school supplies to another family in exchange for home renovations. You can swap houses, vacation condos, cars, laptops, and other devices on many websites like Craigslist. I recently swapped my ancient desktop Mac (from the first line of Macs ever made) for a desk lamp, via Kijiji, a subsidiary of eBay's site in Canada similar to Craigslist (the word "kijiji" means "village" in Swahili). The person who wanted my Mac was a collector of the first line of these fruit colored machines, now considered so clunky and slow. He was missing the turquoise one from his collection. Who would have thought I would find possibly the one person in my town with such a need, and that he would have a desk lamp I wanted?

One popular exchange is called U-exchange.com. Here, traders are categorized by location – of course, trades are typically easier when done locally. A variation on straight barter is something called "indirect trade." In this instance, users of a network or system earn credit by selling goods and services for either "community dollars" or "trade dollars," and are then entitled to goods or services (not necessarily similar) but equivalent in value to what they have earned in the network. In 1991, in Ithaca, New York, home of Cornell University, a group instituted its own currency, "Ithaca Hours." Despite its name, this group doesn't use time-based currency, but rather, actual paper currency. It can only be spent within the network on approved goods and services. Members earn units by selling their goods and services. All currency is calculated as fractions of an hour. Members of Ithaca Hours set their own prices as they would for a common currency. This network is still in operation today, and its organizers say several million dollars worth of Ithaca Hours have been traded since its beginnings – keeping the value in the local economy.

TIME-BANKS

Some networks use a time-based currency as the units of exchange. These exchanges have started up in the U.S., Canada, Britain, and at least 20 other countries. The currency is called "time dollars" – individuals accumulate these by performing various services within the network. This practice can be tricky, though, since everyone's time earns the same rate of credit, regardless of education, experience, or expertise. This would seem to be a disadvantage for professionals like doctors, lawyers, web designers, and consultants, but many of these professionals set aside a portion of their time for charitable work – they offer their services for time credits, and it allows members who couldn't otherwise afford these services to get them with time credits they've earned doing what they *can* offer.

One of the oldest and largest of the community time banks is the "Hour Exchange" in Portland, Maine. Founded in 1997, it now has 700 active members providing more than 1600 services in 178 categories. The group's focus is on community service – time dollars can be spent on local cultural activities like theater, ballet, music, and other art forms. Two hours of service gets you a ticket to a two-hour performance. The idea for time banks has gained interest, and other such groups have formed around the country and across the world. Major credit is given to Edgar S. Cahn, co-founder of the National Legal Services Program and founder of the Antioch School of Law. He founded TimeBanks USA (www.timebanks.org), a network of networks, listing approximately 60 active time-bank non-profit organizations in the U.S. and about 30 others around the world.

USING RESOURCES INSTEAD OF SCARCE CASH: *YOU CAN TRADE WHAT YOU DO, HAVE, AND KNOW*

There are many barter companies or exchanges currently doing business in person, on the phone, or, more and more nowadays, online. One large such company, Revenu.biz, located mostly in the Southeast, offers a huge list of companies that provide products and services to its members. "It all started with a 'wish list'," said Karen Roumay, one of the company's founders. "If a member who was a printing company needed someone to clean its offices, we would sign up a cleaning service," Roumay explained. From there it grew to its current roster of hundreds of members who each have an account of what they call "alternative currency." Another network, MidWest Barter Exchange, also has hundreds of small businesses as members, who are encouraged to do their business within the exchange. They accumulate "exchange dollars" or "scrip," which can be used on any product or service within the network.

Now there's a new form of alternative currency called Bitcoin. It is the first form of digital currency (also called "cryptocurrency"). The system is peer-to-peer; users can transact directly without needing an intermediary. In the barter exchanges described above, the way the money works differs among the different exchanges. In most, members pay a one-time membership fee, plus a monthly administration fee, and then a percentage of each transaction goes to the network. There doesn't seem to be any hard and fast rule about the fees or the commissions – in some networks, the seller is charged a transaction fee; in others, it's the buyer who pays it. Some have given me examples of a split, the commission shared equally between the 2 members of the transaction. A few businesses I know habitually use barter on a regular basis, without joining a formal barter network. Sometimes, barter is conducted more informally by individuals or businesses that see a one-time opportunity for swapping goods and services with each other.

In my own training and consulting business, I often conduct seminars on Business Communications and Influence in a local hotel. The largest expense involved is the price of the meeting room and the catering for breakfast and lunch breaks. Often, I will contact the General Manager of the hotel and offer several seats to members of their staff (placing a retail dollar value on each seat) in exchange for the room and the food. No money is exchanged, they get a valuable seminar for several of their employees – I get a venue and refreshments. Future possibilities for this relationship: they might invite us to teach the seminar for all of their employees, I might recommend their facility to my corporate or organizational clients.

Additionally, when I was attending Empire State University in New York City, a group of us came up with the vision of a trip to India to study the status of women there. We already had our leaders lined up – the Canadian anthropologist, Barbara, and our professor. Barbara's area of specialty was Tibet, and more specifically Tibetan Buddhist nuns. Our professor was an Indian psychologist who had worked for the Fulbright Foundation and had many high level contacts in India in business and government. I wrote a grant proposal to the State of New York, requesting funding for the group trip. I also was asked to be the scribe for the group during the trip. We got the grant. In exchange for my efforts, I got a stipend to defray my expenses. During the trip we met so many influential people that I was able to stay for many months after the group went home to conduct my own research and write articles for local Indian magazines.

Another example of trading my writing or other expertise was when I was finishing graduate school in my new field, Organizational Development (OD). I was an older student and had plenty of catching up to do in the practical application of the theories we were learning at university. I knew I wasn't ready to go out into the world and market myself as a "practitioner." I needed practice. At a conference, I met Neale, a partner in one of the leading OD firms at that time. As we chatted, he revealed that one of the other partners, Peter, was writing a book but needed serious help in streamlining and editing the manuscript. I jumped at the opportunity. In return, they offered to include me in client conferences and give me "floor time" to interact with the client groups and hone my skills. This was a wonderful chance to train from the masters in the field, and I took full advantage of it. I enjoyed editing the book (which indeed needed plenty of editing) and it went on to become a big success. However, I didn't get credit in the "Acknowledgements" section for my contribution. This taught me that, when bartering, one must be very specific regarding what you want and what you are prepared to give.

Right now, I'm writing this chapter from the spacious veranda of my villa at a beautiful hotel in the rain forest in Jamaica (while back home in Canada, winter storms rage and temperatures plummet to Arctic levels). I am the guest of good friends of mine who are developing this property as an eco-resort – they have elicited my advice on how to position and market it to the growing ecology-minded audience in the U.S. and Canada. I have traded my consulting services for a stay at this beautiful place, as well as a week at their other boutique hotel in another town.

Several years ago, I was living and working in New York, feeling stressed and burned out. I heard about a fabulous spa, Rancho La Puerta, located just south of San Diego, in Baja California. I approached the Program Directors and proposed that I would conduct a few seminars on Goal Setting and Time Management (very much needed by too-busy and stressed people – their customers). They agreed, and, instead of paying me a fee, we bartered – 4 days and nights of complimentary stay for me for every 2-hour seminar I put on. A great deal! I did a few sessions and got to stay for over a week. The work was not at all taxing, since these were topics that I taught to executives in my everyday practice back home (although not in leotards and sandals). Some speakers do this with Cruise Ships and other vacation destinations. It's nice work, if you can get it, but, of course one must remember, you can't pay your rent with room night credits at exotic resorts.

As we've seen, barter is an age-old practice and continues to this day. We seem to have a natural instinct for "trade". Once we begin the practice, even in small forms, we are likely to become stimulated and more creative in the ways we can swap, exchange, trade our own resources for others which we need.

Resources

Very succinct article about the "history of money" with a great info-graphic compiled by Bartercard:

- http://www.telegraph.co.uk/finance/businessclub/money/11174013/The-history-of-money-from-barter-to-bitcoin.html

---

5.

The Peer Mentor Model: A 21st Century Version of an Age-Old Practice

We all have an exquisite ledger or balance sheet in which we tally who owes what to whom. We do this every day with countless people in our lives, but not necessarily in ways that are purposeful or conscious. Business is based on a complex arrangement of favors. Yet we do not always make these debits and credits explicit to one another. Therein often lies the disappointment. We have varying expectations (but do not articulate them) and then different levels of fulfillment or lack thereof. The important point is that it is a way to maximize your own resources and use the resources of others all around you. They are available abundantly if you will just look—and ask.

Peer Mentorship, the process (of identifying your strengths and areas of improvement, and then pairing up with another for mutual support) can reduce the feelings of inadequacy and competition we *all* have. Now you can look at someone else's competence as potential help, assistance, and support for you. I also have called this process, "re-source-ing,"

Re-source-ing is when you use your own resources and those of others to achieve leverage and synergy for all to succeed. Peer Mentoring is the method by which you and a partner help each other out in complementary ways. We all have a need to have a champion, a sponsor, a supporter. This is not necessarily in the form of a boss or even a superior but the person will be senior to you (more knowledgeable, more experienced) in a particular skill or resource area. An important difference between Peer Mentoring and other types of support is that this is explicit and specific, rather than random. It is based on complementary skills, resources and needs. This relationship is not necessarily connected to friendship or personal feelings but a business contract, a bargain. While in a sense it is cooler and more distant than friendship, in other ways it's more committed and intimate than other relationships. You are committed to someone else's success as they are to yours, and you are offering your gifts to each other.

At a recent conference "The Organization Woman" I ran the opening session for 150 women using this Peer-Mentor model. The feedback has been overwhelming. When Working Woman Magazine ran a one-paragraph description of the workshop, I was flooded with inquiries from readers all over the country asking for more information. My own research with control and experimental groups shows dramatic improvement in goal achievement when individuals use the technique. As a professor of management at Montclair State University in New Jersey, I used the Peer-Mentor pairings as a technique to help the students achieve their learning goals in a specific topic. The students reported that using the process gave them focus and support towards achieving those goals.

I had heard about the exciting work of Barbara Sher, whose books first described the "Women's Success Teams." In this process, aspiring career women formed small teams and assessed what each member had to offer and needed from the other team members. I felt, however, that while I like the principles of the teams, the process would be more focused and specific if it was carried out with just two people. There are many aids and catalysts to success. The Peer-Mentor process is one that I (and by now thousands of others) have found to be most effective. It's a way of combining two very powerful ideas –

networking and mentoring – into a daily ongoing support system, whatever business or career you're engaged in.

We all do favors and have implicit bargains with one another. You help me out when I have a problem, and I owe you one. We rarely discuss these hidden contracts with one another, although most people have an exquisitely delicate set of mental balance scales in these matters. Sometimes these balances do not get discussed, and one person feels ripped off, exploited, as if she has been doing most of the giving and not getting enough back. In the most common definitions, a mentor can perform the role of a teacher, a sponsor, a role model, a counselor, or a true believer (later in this chapter, we'll discuss the various definitions of "Mentor" given by Daniel Levinson, noted psychologist). The Peer-Mentor system focuses on many of these ingredients. Yet there is the element of mutual exchange, which is the dominant theme in the system.

The value in these exchanges is that they are not necessarily about friendship, having a great time together, or even about being similar. In fact, the agreement can often work better when there are differences – complementary differences between the people. That is, I am better at A than you are, and you are better at B than I am – I will help you learn A if you help me learn B, and we both wind up with more or better quality than we had when alone. The value at the core of this relationship is that it is slightly more impersonal than friendship but more committed than friendships usually are. That is, the two people have a bargain (a contractual agreement) not to like or love one another, but to support and assist one another in achieving their separate goals. Their common goal is for both people to achieve their separate goals.

There is an objectivity and coolness about this. Less charge is involved than in a friendship, yet it is much warmer than a strictly business relationship. For example, if you ask me, I will give you a critique on how you handled that business telephone call I overheard in a manner that is objective and constructive. The Peer Mentor's purpose is to enhance your style in your business communications so that you are more effective and productive, thereby increasing your chances of achieving the goal you have articulated in your contract with your partner.

Your partner will be attentive to your behaviors that are counter productive, off-purpose, or taking you away from your goal. In this Peer-Mentor contract you have spelled out, your partner's obligation and commitment to you includes telling you how you may be helping or hindering yourself. You establish a relationship with someone who contractually is committed to your success and accomplishment. The agreement or contract you design sets up a way for you to get feedback, support, tutoring, sponsorship, contacts, criticism, or whatever else you may have asked for help with

Most of us have a great sense of appropriateness in gift giving. The lavishness, the originality, the regularity of gifts we give one another for holidays, birthdays, anniversaries, etc. is a finely entrenched, carefully constructed norm of reciprocity that has usually developed over the years in our relationships. I may usually spend half a day creating and designing a personal collage for your birthday card – making it the most uniquely personal and special kind of gift. If you send me a dime store item a few times in a row, I may be painfully reluctant to invest my time, love, and creativity in you the next time around.

We have all kinds of implicit agreements and act on them every day of our lives. We also exercise balances of reciprocity in business activities. A kind of "you scratch my back, I'll scratch yours" pervades almost every organizational system. In fact, most successful executives cite a network of contacts, personal and business accounts of debts and favors as important keys to their success. The "old boy network ," the informal fraternity in most old line organizations, is a prime example of this. Successful business people have learned these networking skills very early in their careers – how to use other people as resources. Unfortunately, using people often has a pejorative connotation, but people who practice this in the way we are discussing know that there is nothing exploitive intended – they are receiving as much as they're giving.

When I go to Kansas City and need three or four contacts there, I can call one of my contacts who will give me the information I need. I will not need to remind her that when she needed publishing contacts and a place to stay in New York, I came up with both for her. Next time, it will be her turn to ask me for something. These favors won't ever be recorded in an actual ledger, yet we both know what the score is. People who are experienced at this game will be acutely aware when the score needs to be evened up. If the last three times we have had contact, my friend has done something for me, I am likely to go out of my way to think about how I can do something for her. I know that if I do not, the abundant flow of generosity she is sending my way may dry up.

In writing this book, I was active in an interesting exchange of favors. My friend and colleague, an anthropologist, called me for moral support and inspiration for a project that was giving her problems. She had received a grant and a story assignment to go to Tibet (her area of study) to write a story on reciprocity in an agricultural commune. The problem was that she was not able to get a green light from the Chinese agricultural commissioner in Beijing to enter Tibet. A friend of mine, an international businessman from Washington D.C., had recently told me about his forthcoming trip to China and a new trend in international business – barter and countertrade. This is a system of trade in which no money is exchanged, rather, countries make deals to swap goods and services with each other, an update of the old system of barter that has been with us for centuries. I was aware that he had some needs for writing expertise.

I introduced them to each other, and he has since promised to use his influence with the Chinese (he knows the agricultural commissioner) to help her get into Tibet. In exchange for this favor, she has agreed to ghostwrite an article about his international activities in this area. When her own project is completed, she will stay on in China to develop the story about his work. Because I facilitated this meeting, she has agreed to help me with some basic research for the chapter on "Reciprocity: An Historical and Anthropological Perspective" for this book. Doing the research and writing of that chapter myself would have taken me weeks, and because I was able to introduce and help two friends, I was able to save myself considerable time and energy . So everybody is happy. She gets into China, he gets an article about his business, and I get professional research and and advice for my book. Next time around, our needs will stimulate other creative ways we can be of use to each other.

When it came to the final version of this book that you are reading, I teamed up with the very talented and learned Dr. Gabriela Djerrahian, professor of Anthropology at UQAM in Montreal who wrote Chapter 2, "The Gift: Rituals of Exchange and contract"

In another example of this reciprocal system, an acquaintance, a high school English teacher, wanted to learn to parlay her skill of teaching writing into a more lucrative activity. She wanted to teach writing seminars for business people. This is one of the areas I work in as a management consultant. Last week we spent a morning together and I gave her a two-hour briefing on the pros and cons of doing this work as a business by sharing my experiences of successes and failures. In return, she agreed to write and edit some brochures I have been unable to complete for the last several months.

We may run into problems when she starts her business and is a competitor. I have a few choices. On the one hand, I could withhold information from her for fear of the competition possibly stealing potential clients and diminishing a source of livelihood for me. On the other hand, I could tell her everything I know, train her as an apprentice, and develop more of my own business so that as she becomes more experienced, we could be associates and share the client load. My past experience lets me know that once I have become more competent, confident, and successful at something, I felt abundant, generous, and more willing to share. I get a vision of the abundance of clients, business, opportunities, and money out there. When I feel insecure, I feel threatened and see everyone as a threat. By being clear about what I want in return from her, I diminished the threat factor. Consequently, we both increased our competence. Over time we discovered that formalizing these agreements created a unique method for achieving both short-term and long-term goals. The method evolved out of our own needs and has changed greatly based on our shifting interests and concerns. Some of our method includes the most vital aspects of a mentor relationship.

What is a mentor exactly? Usually she is a person of greater experience and seniority in the world than the protégé with whom she is entering into a partnership. A mentor can be a teacher, a sponsor, a role model, a counselor, or a true believer –someone who's always in your corner, cheering you on. Daniel Levinson, noted psychologist, describes the various functions of these labels:

Teacher – to enhance the skills and intellectual development of the student/protégée

Sponsor – to use her influence in the culture, organization, or milieu into which the protégée needs entry or advancement.

Host or Guide – to welcome the novice into a new social or cultural world, profession, or organization; schooling her in social rituals, initiations, values, customs, cast of characters, politics, or protocols.

Exemplar – to serve as a role model after whom the protégé can model herself.

Counselor or Advisor – to coach the protégé through situations new or stressful; the mentor can give concrete advice and suggestions based on her broader or longer experience.

True Believer – to believe in the protégé's dream, her competence in fulfilling them, and her right to achieve it. In this role, the mentor is an encourager, a cheerer-on, a guide, helping the protégé's sometimes flagging confidence and spirit. This may be the most important mentor role.

Many 'how to succeed' books suggest that we each need a mentor. Although a mentor can be a valuable asset, the suggestion has a number of flaws in its application, namely:

1. There are not enough skilled, successful people higher up in the success ladder who are both willing and able to help each of us.

2. The method keeps people stuck in the 'Pygmalion' or savior fantasy that someone 'up there' will take care of us.

3. There is an imbalance between the receiver and the giver. The mentee is always in a debt or obligation because the mentor is doing all the giving.

4. The process contributes to ignoring the value of people at our own level who have considerable resources to offer.

5. Much of what happens depends on the mentor's personality, her amount of self-esteem. Some mentors are only interested in doing mentoring because of their own narcissism – they need the constant reinforcement of a superior position. Others are very controlling and do not hear or have much empathy for the needs and concerns of the protégé.

Betty Harragan, author of the seminal management book for women, *Games Mother Never Taught You*, asserts that there is a dangerous emphasis on mentoring these days. One concern is that women will clutch at the idea of getting a mentor to help them navigate their way up the corporate ladder and renounce responsibility for their own progress. An article in "Savvy Magazine" in the late 1980's by Kathleen Fury calls it "Mentor Mania -The Search for Mr. Right Goes to the Office." Here the danger is based on the idea that someone else (a daddy, godfather, fairy godmother) can set your life right and help you get what you want. Only recently has it been possible for women to even have female mentors. However, most women found when looking for a mentor that there were few successful women around who could qualify as mentors. If there were, they often had a Queen Bee attitude of "I've made it on my own and struggled through - you have to go it alone."

The issue of competition still seems to be quite strong among women, and often a woman who is in a position to groom and mentor a younger, less experienced one may feel threatened as the apprentice becomes as proficient and competent as she is. Women have not been at the upper rungs of organizations long enough to feel automatically comfortable and secure there. The idea of bright, young, assertive women moving in and up can be a disturbing one to some women who feel as though there are only a few spots carved out for women at the top.

Other reasons women are cautious or reluctant to become sponsors or mentors to other women are that they feel as though they must keep their hands – and the record – clean. They may do themselves political and career damage if male colleagues and bosses think they are too prejudiced or aligned with women. Another reason is that mentoring takes time and work, and successful career women often believe they do not have much time to spend on this task. Lastly, some women who have had male mentors believe that younger women would be better off doing the same. Men still have more clout, more power, and more expertise in a majority of areas. Some women, however, like other members of oppressed minorities who have long been tokens and have struggled to get "in," feel a moral obligation to help other women. They may also believe that as more women gain entry and success in the organization, the norms can change to make life easier for the ones who got there first. The competitive attitude, although it still exists, seems to have softened in many circles as evidenced by the women's support networks and groups that proliferate.

In many 'how to succeed' books, both men and women did report, however, that they had a number of helping relationships throughout their careers. These relationships, although not necessarily having the intensity of the mentor relationship described earlier, involved mutual respect and a considerable amount of helping, advising, and counseling. Some mentioned that they identified one person who does a particular thing very well and set out to learn this from her or him. In this situation, they are using the mentor as a tutor – going after a particular skill or expertise that the other person has. What our Peer Mentor system focuses on has many of these ingredients in its form. Yet there is the element of *mutual* exchange, which is the dominant theme in the system.

What are the ingredients in the Peer-Mentor process? You can trade what you do, have, and know

1. Each person identifies at least one 'resource' – a skill, an expertise, contacts, etc. that she feels she wants from someone else and one resource she is willing to share.

2. The parties make an agreement to use each other's resource to benefit each other.

3. Each commits herself to the other person's achieving her goal and becoming successful, despite the fact that they may experience jealousy, envy, competition, or threat if that does happen.

4. The posture of a Peer Mentor is to keep the other on target, to help push through the fears, blocks, and procrastination, and to believe in the other even when they do not believe in themselves.

5. Each agrees to receive the support, counsel, sponsorship, and advice that is designed in the contract. Each agrees to give what the partner considers a fair trade. The deal may not be in the same currency or area of expertise. Each will try to be explicit and specific in describing clearly what they expect of each other and how they know when they are living up to their ends of the exchange.

6. The feedback they give each other will focus on being objective, specific, and critical of the behaviors or activities that seem counter-productive, not the whole person.

7. The goals and objectives of each partner in the contract are spelled out clearly and explicitly so they each know what the other means. For example, the goal "To get more satisfaction and responsibility from my job" is not explicit or clear enough. How will you know when that's happened? How will your Peer Mentor know that you've accomplished it?

8. They will design strategies, activities, or the vehicle to reach these goals. The goals are the 'what,' the strategies or activities are the 'how.'

9. The Peer Mentor role could take a number of forms. For example, one of the peers may be more politically savvy than the other and might help her peer figure out which projects would get her the most visibility. She may help you score the most political points with your supervisor or other people who have some say over your career and your salary review. Similarly, her peer mentor could help her rehearse the talk she will have when she sits down with her boss.

The peer/mentor model is based on the idea that pairs have an investment in and commitment to one another. That there will undoubtedly be conflict is seen as a natural and normal corollary of an intimate, committed, and involved relationship. In all our research on human relations, the working through of this kind of conflict or difficulty seems to help strengthen the commitment and interest of the two people, so, in a way, these conflicts are simultaneously positive for the relationship.

This description of the Peer Mentor model may seem a bit complicated, but in practice it is actually pretty simple, as you'll see in the detailed instructions in the next few chapters. I wanted to give you as thorough and detailed a road map as possible, but you may improvise and experiment until you find the process that works for you.

6.

PEER MENTOR: A UNIQUE PARTNERSHIP CHARACTERISTICS AND COMPARISONS

The chart in this chapter enables us to define the Peer-Mentor relationship and to provide an in-depth discussion of that relationship. Each aspect of the relationship is defined (i.e., power, competition, commitment, etc.), and then compared and contrasted with the Peer-Mentor dyad in each dimension with other known dyadic relationships, i.e. Mentor/Protégée, Friends, Business Partners, Teacher/Student, and parent/child.

The representation I used here is that of the traditional Western parent-and-child relationship. Parents can and do influence children in many ways, by example, rewards and punishments, moral guidelines, and rules.

Now I will direct your attention to the chart on the following page as we go through its various elements. In the Peer-Mentor relationship, Competition is likely and expected. When that is acknowledged, it is discussed and used to enhance the relationship. In terms of Trust, the goal is to have a high level of trust between the Peer Mentors, as it is the foundation for a strong and productive relationship between the participants. The column of Dependency refers to an interdependent relationship. The Purpose is to assist the growth and development (and advance the goals) of each person in the Peer-Mentor relationship. In terms of the Selection Based On, the selection criteria are based on complementary skills, resources, and needs.

Commitment is based on a contract and is always renegotiable. The Balance of Giving–Reciprocity is shared; each offers skills or resources to meet the other's needs. The Currency being exchanged is that of skills, support, resources, and encouragement. Exclusivity does not necessarily apply to peer mentors as it does to other dyads.

According to their goals, individuals can have many Peer Mentors whose 'haves' and 'needs are consistent with theirs. What could End or Threaten the Relationship? In the case of the Peer Mentor, the relationship is threatened or may end if either violates the letter or the spirit of the agreement (e.g., breaks confidentiality or works against the peer mentor in some way). However, more positively, the relationship might end if or when both members have achieved their stated goals. If you review the chart and the other pair relationships we explore, you will see how they are similar to or different from the unique Peer Mentor relationship.

≠	Power	Competition	Trust
PEER/ MENTOR	Shared; each has power in specific area	Expected, discussed, and used to enhance relationship	High
Parent/ Child	Parent has most	Often covert	Varies
Siblings	Unequal	Common, open	Varies
Friends	Shared	Common, often covert	Varies
Spouses	Shared	Frequent, often covert	Implicit; varies
Lovers	Shared	Explicit – low Implicit –high	Varies
Mentor/ Protégé	Unequal	Low	High
Teacher/Student (Coach/Player)	Unequal	Low	Student usually trusts teacher/ coach
Consultant/ Doctor/ Therapist & Clients	Unequal; "professional" has expert power, client has hire/fire power	Low	Varies; should be high for relationship effectiveness
Business Partners	Implicit – equal	Often high and covert	Explicit – high; Implicit – varies

≠	Dependency	Purpose	Selection Based on
PEER/ MENTOR	Interdependent	To help growth and development of each	Different goals; complement-ary skills, and needs
Parent/ Child	Child depends on parent; later reverse	To raise and develop child	No selection; exc. adoption
Siblings	Mutual; sometimes unequal	Continuation of family relationships	Birth
Friends	Implicit-equal sometimes unequal	Personal support/ Companion-ship, fulfill-ment	Similar values, goals, or interests
Spouses	Often unequal	To enhance each other's lives, raise family	Similar or complement-ary values; attraction
Lovers	Explicit– equal Implicit– unequal	To enhance each other's lives	Shared interests, attraction
Mentor/ Protégé	Protégé dependent on mentor	To "groom" and develop protégé	Protégé's needs Mentor's need to be needed
Teacher/Student (Coach/Player)	Student dependent on teacher/coach	To teach, develop student	Student's need
Consultant/ Doctor/ Therapist & Clients	Client dependent on professional; prof. needs client for livelihood	To "heal," counsel, help, or advise the client	Consultant selected for expertise, empathy, chemistry
Business Partners	Interdependent	Shared purposes & goals; work, productivity and money	Shared goals; complement ary skills

≠	**Commitment**	**Balance of Giving and Reciprocity**	**Currency**
PEER/ MENTOR	Contractual; renegotiable	Shared – each gives skills or resources to meet other's needs	Skills, support, resources
Parent/ Child	Permanent, emotional, and financial	Early – parent does most; Later– shared	Love, support loyalty, money
Siblings	Permanent, emotional	Explicit – equal, implicit – often unequal	Love, support
Friends	Long-term, emotional	Explicit – equal, implicit – often unequal	Love, favors
Spouses	Long-term, legal, emotional, and financial	Explicit – equal, implicit – often unequal	Love, support, money, time, sex
Lovers	Emotional, sometimes financial	Each offers different "gifts" to other	Love, support, time, sex, (money?)
Mentor/ Protégé	Implicit, sometimes explicit	Mentor is "giver"	Mentor – experience, skill; Protégé – loyalty, admiration
Teacher/Student (Coach/Player)	Implicit; sometimes explicit	Teacher is "giver"	Teacher – knowledge; Student – loyalty
Consultant/ Doctor/ Therapist & Clients	Long- or short-term contractual	Professional gives expertise; client gives fees	Expertise, money
Business Partners	Contractual; legal, financial	Equal, implicit	Money, skills, loyalty

≠	**Exclusivity**	**Factors that Could End or Threaten Relationships**
PEER/ MENTOR	No. An individual can have many peer/mentors	Either violates agreements in contracts
Parent/ Child	Child only 1 set; parents may have many	Death, Divorce
Siblings	In particular sibling relationships	Death, Estrangement
Friends	Not usually	Violation of explicit or implicit pacts
Spouses	Yes – in traditional form	Violation of explicit of implicit pacts, e.g. Adultery
Lovers	Yes – in traditional form	Violation of explicit or implicit norms, pacts
Mentor/ Protégé	Not necessarily	Protégé no longer needs mentor; mentor feels threatened by competition from Protégé
Teacher/Student (Coach/Player)	No	Students completes education; player or coach violates pacts
Consultant/ Doctor/ Therapist & Clients	Not usually, except in conflict of interest	Professional. does not deliver services or violate norms; implicit or explicit agreements
Business Partners	Usually, at least in "primary" business	Violation of explicit or implicit (moral) agreements

7.

Goals

Until one is committed there is hesitating,
the chance to draw back, always ineffectiveness.

Concerning all acts of initiative (and creation)
there is one elementary truth, the ignorance of which kills
countless ideas and splendid plans:

The moment one definitely
commits oneself, Providence moves too.

All sorts of things occur to help one,
that would never otherwise have occurred.

A whole stream of events issues from the decision,
raising in one's favor all manner of unforeseen incidents
and meetings and material assistance which no man could
have dreamed would have come his way

—Goethe

ACHIEVING YOUR GOALS

When you set a goal, it thereafter acts like a magnet; you are pulled towards it. The resources you need along the way, which you previously thought were inaccessible, now contribute to your momentum. These resources also are being pulled towards a similar goal. But notice, for a magnet to work best, the object being attracted should not have to take unnecessary detours. Yet, along the way, other magnets may draw the magnet off of its goal-oriented path. This is similar to how goal setting and achieving works for people, too. There are often obstacles, oftentimes, monetary ones, that demand your cooperation on your path to your goals. In fact, the winding road toward your goals may seem, at times, to be headed in the wrong direction. But going with the flow can be an efficient way to reach your goal. The traveler seeking directions may be told by the native, "You can't get there from here;" he doesn't mean you can't reach your goal but that a straight path to that particular goal is not practical. Instead, you may have to backtrack before going forward, or you have to go somewhere else first. But, unless your goal is unrealistic, it CAN be reached.

When the exercise instructor says "No pain, no gain," she is not saying that pain is the goal, but that there is always some unavoidable price to pay for progress. However, whatever unpleasant side effects you may have during the process, they need not create a struggle or even slow down your progress. On the contrary, the 'burn' one experiences when exercising, for example, can act as a helpful barometer for judging one's progress.

NO PAIN NO GAIN

The fear of discomfort is too easily a rationalization for making no effort at all Unpleasant side effects distract and discourage a poorly motivated person, but these side effects can actually be turned into opportunities. If you choose to strive to achieve your goals with this attitude, it can take your life from a level which is diffused, like the light from an ordinary electric bulb, to a level which is powerful and concentrated, like that of a laser. Setting goals and objectives are especially important at the start of a trip. Yogi Berra said "When you don't know where you are going, it is hard to tell when you get there." Conversely, when you do know where you're going, getting there is a whole lot easier. A set of objectives creates a clear pathway, which frees you from a whole spectrum of worries and uncertainties.

When you know what you'd like to do or have in the future, you can start preparing logically instead of hoping things will take care of themselves. No one can predict the future, but the better prepared you are for some eventuality, the more confident you'll feel about dealing with whatever life hands you. Learn to recognize that goals and objectives are tools to help you, not trap you. The distinction between goals and objectives is an important one. On the one hand, objectives are a lifetime, ongoing direction. A goal, on the other hand, is a specific, achievable, measurable, event or experience. Setting goals helps you measure progress and focus on the activities you're currently involved in, giving you a feeling of movement. One of your objectives might be to help make life better for those less fortunate than yourself. You may never accomplish the objective completely, but you can set some specific goals and plan specific activities, such as: volunteering to work at the children's hospital, or donating money to your favorite charity.

Many people think of goals in vague terms – they say they want to be happier, have more money, or have more leisure time. A better way to use goals is to make them concrete. Ask yourself, exactly how much money do you want to have, where you want to go on vacation, or when you'll be made department manager. This kind of refining and clarifying takes some effort, but it's worth it. Many people are afraid to set goals and objectives. They're afraid of becoming too tied down or afraid they won't be able to reach the standards they've set, but this need not be a deterrent.

YOU CAN ALWAYS CHANGE YOUR GOALS AND OBJECTIVES

The important thing is to start somewhere on something. Successful people achieve because they have a sense of purpose, of direction. They are in control of their lives. If this means altering a goal based on the direction they've started moving, they will. This allows them to continue moving forward, even if it's in a slightly different direction. Unsuccessful people avoid thinking about the future and procrastinate, drifting without direction. Life is controlling them. The following guidelines should be kept in mind when setting goals and objectives to help you be more successful:

1. Goals Should Be Yours - It's all right to accept advice and suggestions from others, but you will be more motivated to do something if it's something you really want to do.

2. Goals Should Be Written - Keeping goals in your head will not work as effectively as writing them down. Besides being clearer, written goals serve as reminders and records.

3. Goals Should Be Realistic and Attainable – A goal is not a fantasy or a daydream. It should be something you can accomplish with some effort and stretching. Don't set goals too low, but if they're too difficult, you won't believe you can accomplish them and will probably never start. Don't be overly optimistic, either.

4. Goals Should Have Target Dates - Give yourself time limits. Often you will have sub-objectives with their own target dates. If you don't make the target, don't hate yourself – just set a new date.

5. Goals Should Be Compatible - Watch out for conflicts. If conflicts exist, working on one goal may prevent you from achieving another, and then you end up stuck all the way around.

6. Goals Are Not Activities - Once you've set some goals, you'll have to figure out some ways to achieve them. Write down the specific activities you must do to achieve a goal by its target date.

As opportunities and obstacles arise, we are often forced to change our goals, but a wise person anticipates the need for change by re-evaluating and renewing goals. You can generate renewed goals periodically in order to stay current with your own internal growth and changes and with the external changes in your work and life. Your goals of a year ago may already be achieved. Or, a major change in your life or career may be the catalyst for you to set new goals. If you've never really thought about goals and objectives, take some time now to do it. Just jot down thoughts as they come into your mind – even if they seem to be just pipe dreams. Write down some goals for the following categories. You don't have to have them in every category, nor do you have to record them in any particular order.

- Personal
- Family
- Social
- Career
- Financial

REWARDS

Reward yourself every time you achieve a goal, cut out a time-waster or resist procrastination. If you promise yourself a reward, be sure to give it to yourself. Here are some cheerful suggestions for rewards: sing a song aloud, read a magazine, have a massage, take a lesson in something, jog, go fishing, adopt a plant, take a bubble bath, read your horoscope. Major achievements deserve a special treat.

GOAL SUCCESS MODEL

At one time or another you have had what you considered to be an outstanding success, that is, you achieved some results that you desired which completely satisfied you. This tool is designed to help you identify and repeat the specific strategy that brought you to those positive results. Once you can recognize a personal success model for yourself, you will be able to reproduce the results you want at will again and again!

Step 1: Looking at the Goal

What specific goal do you want to achieve now? Write out specific statements about

a) How you picture yourself with the goal achieve,

b) What the physical surroundings will be when that goal is achieved,

c) What good feelings you will have at that moment, and

d) The positive things you will say to yourself or hear from others when this goal is achieved

Step 2: Assessing the Motivation to Change

How motivated are you to reach this goal? Circle the letter that most clearly identifies your level of motivation at this time.

A. It really is only a pipe dream.

B. I want to reach the goal, but I believe it is unreachable for me.

C. I think it would be a good idea, but I am uncommitted to it.

D. I want it, but I'm not sure that this is the right time to go for it.

E. I want it, and I see that I am not directing my energies toward it.

F. I want to achieve this goal, yet I hold back because I'm not sure of others' reactions to my achievement.

G. I know I want it, yet it is not clear to me how to achieve it.

H. I know this goal achievement will help me to take the next step forward.

I. I want this goal, and I believe others will benefit along with me.

J. Achieving this goal will change my life! I am willing to take the positive steps needed in order to reach it.

Using the letter you just circled, put an X next to the corresponding statement and read the explanation.

J - No question! You are clear about wanting the goal and seeing the benefits for all involved.

I, H, G - You are strongly motivated yet not sure about proceeding. Apply the confidence you have in other familiar situations to guide you here. You know that if things don't work out you can always change your plan!

F, E, D - You do want to reach your goal, yet you are putting barriers in the way of your commitment. Imagine putting them aside for now and do the rest of this exercise as if the entire world wants you to succeed!

C, B, A - Your motivation is too low to achieve this goal now. Write out another goal that you truly want to achieve at this time.

Step 3: Looking at the Present State

Where are you now in relation to that goal? Write out specifically how you picture yourself now, what the physical setting you currently see yourself in, why you have not reached that goal yet, and the message you hear from yourself and others because that goal is not yet reached.

Step 4: Support for the Present State

What makes it possible for this present state to exist? Circle those statements that most closely match your own answer to this question.

A. I believe that it always has to be this way.

B. I feel unable to make a change now.

C. I do not see myself doing anything differently.

D. I do not get support from others to go ahead.

E. I tried and could not do anything about it.

F. I am looking too hard for answers in the wrong places.

G. I will not try to change until I know it will work out perfectly.

H. I don't feel right about changing.

I. I should have known how to make this change before now.

J. I tell myself not to try too hard.

K. I feel confused about what is really going on.

L. I feel bored.

M. I know things could have been better if only I had done something else.

Step 5: Moving to the Desired State

Look at each statement you circled. Now write out the counter-statement to each one, using your own positive statements; write them each 10 times, using an extra sheet of paper if necessary. You may want to use the following, which corresponds to the statements in Step 4 as a guide to forming your own statements.

Examples:

a) I believe that situations can always improve.

b) I feel completely enthusiastic and capable of a change now.

c) I clearly see myself doing many new things.

d) I can always generate support from those important to me to encourage my moving ahead.

e) Whenever I try to, I can improve a situation.

f) I easily find alternatives in the most obvious or surprising places.

g) I can try to change even though I may feel awkward at first.

h) I feel excited about changes.

i) When I look at the past, I see how many times I am grateful for the choices I made.

j) I tell myself that I trust my ability to push forward in the most appropriate ways.

k) I am excited and curious about what is really going on.

l) I think I understand what is going on, and I feel delighted with that knowledge inside of me.

m) I am grateful that I chose the paths I did and know I can make even better decisions now.

Step 6: Reaching the Desired Goal

Based on your statements and work in Step 5, what would you need to happen next to let you know you have reached your goal? What would you have to see yourself doing, and how would the physical surroundings need to be? What feelings will you experience then, as well as what positive messages will you hear from yourself and others important to you? Use your creativity and imagination!

Step 7: Flexibility – the Key to the Goal

Think about how many different ways in the past you have successfully solved problems in order to get what you want. Describe below three or four different approaches you can take to move you toward your current goal. Suppose my goal is ask my boss for and get a raise in salary: I could create a chart or other graphic illustrations to show my boss why the raise I am asking for is appropriate, I could cite several examples of companies where people in positions like mine are all earning more than I am, I could write a chronological history of my achievements for the company, or I could show a spreadsheet of my actions on the job and how much money they have saved for the company.

Example 1:

Example 2:

Example 3:

Step 8: Finding the Key that Fits

As you look back at your responses to Step 7, which one seems most likely to help you achieve your current goal? Here you want to work out a step-by-step plan to reach your current goal. Those successful methods that produced past successes can be applied here. As you work through the steps, however, you will probably find yourself fine-tuning the process you used in the past, adjusting for the new goal, for who you are now, or for the different people and environments you are dealing with this time. But your strategy will most likely be the same or at least very similar.

The first step is:

____

____

To be accomplished by (Date)

____

The second step is: (Date)

____

The third step is: (Date)

____

The fourth step is: (Date)

____

Step 9: Success!

At this step you will want to review all the previous steps and transfer to your calendar the dates you indicated in Step 8. Achieving a goal takes planning a strategy and being able to visualize the outcome you want. It takes being able to shift gears and plans if the approach you are using is not working well. Keep in mind that if you don't know what the guideposts are along the way, you will never know if you are moving in the right direction! Repeat these steps for continued success!

GOAL SETTING EXERCISE

Here is an exercise that will help you formulate a well-stated goal. Some of the following goal statements are stated correctly according to our guidelines, and some are not. Write your reaction to each statement. Write in the changes you feel are necessary then read our commentary on each that follows.

1. To give up smoking.
2. To lose weight by July 15.
3. To read one novel a month for the next twelve months, spending no more than five hours a week, at a cost not to exceed $100.

Commentary:

1. To give up smoking - Obviously, you will need, at the very least, a target date. It would be better to say, "To give up smoking by January 16." If you need to involve products or programs that incur some expenses, you could say, for example, "To give up smoking by January 16, and spend the $100 workshop fee necessary to do so."

2. To lose weight by July 15. You must identify how much weight you want to lose. It would be better to say "To lose 5 pounds by February 7." As with the smoking example, include cost factors if necessary.

3. To read one novel a month, spending no more than five hours a week, for the next twelve months, at a cost not to exceed $100 – This goal as stated is acceptable; however, listing which novels you plan to read might be typical of the kind of detailed planning we discuss next.

SETTING PRIORITIES

Setting priorities simply means deciding the order in which you want to accomplish certain tasks. You set priorities everyday of your life. What you do is determine that it is more practical to make a grocery list before going to the supermarket or realize that it makes more sense to take a course in accounting, so you can be prepared for – or attract – a promotion. Look over your list of goals and decide which items are of the highest priority for you. Pick the two goals in this top category and put an "A" next to them. Pick the next two most important items and label them "B." Now pick those goals that will be in your "C" category, those that are goals, but are the least important to you at this time. You can, of course, break them down further: A-1, A-2, B-1, B-2, and so forth. Use this list to set goals for five years, one year, and six months. The chart on the next page will help you set objectives for all areas of your life.

Remember, goals must be specific, concrete, and measure-able. Yes, this is work, but to get what you want from life, you must first know specifically what that is and what to do to get it. This exercise will help you find out what is important to you. Setting goals gets easier with practice. Like most things, the first time is the hardest. The good news is that most people who do it swear that there is something magical about it. Just writing down goals has something to do with making them happen. Your desires and dreams are valuable, and they could be realized – but not if they remain top secret, perhaps even to yourself. As you can see in the below chart, each category applies to an area of your life. As specifically as you can, write down what you would like to be, do, or have for each category.

	5 YEARS	1 YEAR	6 MONTHS
Money			
Career			
Income			
Intimate Relationships			
Friends			
Family			
Residence			
Transportation			
Travel			
Material Possessions			
Recreation			
Health			
Spiritual			
Education			

Given your present life and circumstances, goals should be realistic and attainable, as we've stated before. Objectives might be lofty, or sound too grandiose, but you are setting a direction in which to focus your energies.

1. Money - How much would you like to be earning in five years? How much money would you like to have saved? Be specific – write the dollar amount.
2. Career - What title, job function, or responsibilities would you like to have?
3. Intimate relationships - Would you like to be married? Single? Have children?
4. Social relationships - Would you like to have more friends? End some relationships? Change the quality of some friendships?
5. Family relationships - Would you like to improve communication with your mother? Have clearer understandings with your children?
6. Residence - Would you like to buy a house? Sell the one you have? Live in the country? Redecorate?
7. Transportation - Would you like a new car in five years? What kind? What color? Get rid of a car and join a car-sharing service?
8. Travel - Where would you like to visit? For how long? With whom?
9. Material possessions - What would you like to acquire in five years? A new smartphone? New furniture? Designer clothes? What would you like to get rid of?
10. Recreation - What activities would you like to have as regular fun in your life? Go to the theatre? How often?

11. Body Health - Would you like to lose fifteen pounds? Jog three times a week? Get regular dental checkups?

12. Spiritual - What spiritual practice goals do you have? Meditate every day? Be mindful during meals?

13. Education - Would you like to go back to school? Take a drawing or painting class? Learn to play the guitar?

CREATIVE TENSION

Given your present life and circumstances, goals should be realistic and attainable, as we've stated before. Objectives might be lofty, or sound unrealistic. After you've had some practice with setting and achieving goals, you may find that you will be more confident and want to set higher ones. This adaptability will give you the capability of living with a moderate degree of uncertainty and anxiety (this is called "creative tension"). Success-driven people push *up* toward their goal, rather than lower their goal to a level that is easier to reach. Rather than make the required effort to reach the higher goals, less motivated people settle for more reachable substitute goals. This is entirely up to you. Remember, these are your personal goals, and you can always change and adjust them as you go along. You may find, that once you have thought about, set, and written down goals, you may find interesting opportunities in your path. As Goethe famously said,

> *The moment one definitely commits oneself, Providence moves too. All sorts of things occur to help one, that would never otherwise have occurred. A whole stream of events issues from the decision, raising in one's favor all manner of unforeseen incidents and meetings and material assistance which no man could have dreamed would have come his way.*

8.

How and Where to Find a Peer Mentor

Once you decide that working with a Peer Mentor (or several) will be beneficial to you, where and how will you find one? Well, once you begin looking, you'll find potential "Success Buddies" are all around you! Here is a list of some places that you might find a good Peer Mentor":

1. At your regular job - There may be people around who have different job descriptions or functions, but you may like them and find they have skills that you would like to learn. Be sure not to overlook those in different parts of your organization simply through the everyday workings of your job. Or you might meet people in Inter-department teams or task forces. You might even meet someone at the company's softball team (we will get to non-business activities in just a moment). At these kinds of meetings, you'll have plenty of opportunity to see people's skills and character in action (as well as their deficiencies or flaws). If you do see someone who looks promising you can invite her or him for a meal or coffee to talk about it further. What do you have to lose? If they're not interested in forming a Peer-Mentor relationship with you, you might still make a new friend.

2. In training or professional development meetings - In this kind of setting, you may be meeting people from different organizations or companies, different departments or areas of your own organization, or even countries or states far from your own. You are all learning together, so it's a great way to observe how someone interacts with the instructor, with other students, and what skills or bright spots they exhibit. Again, you can take the initiative to ask the person to sit down with you sometime during the event to discuss this new educational tool you have discovered.

3. Work travel - This could be one of the best opportunities of all – if you go to a conference, there may indeed be some of your colleagues attending, but there will likely be hundreds, maybe even thousands, of other interesting people you don't know. Of course, you may only get to meet a fraction of them, and you'll be able to practice the skill of approaching strangers at pretty low risk because if it doesn't go the way you'd like it to, you'll probably never see them again.

4. Extra-curricular activities - You may find people in settings other than the work or professional spheres. For example, you might meet someone at your place of worship, fundraisers, charitable activities, or informal receptions, All of these give you a chance to observe other people on their 'off' time. You may observe how they interact on a volunteer project team, how they behave one-on-one. Do you participate in team sports, play bridge or Scrabble regularly with the same people, belong to a choir or other musical group, go to a book club, or participate in a trivia group? All of these may present great opportunities to see people in a different light, get to know them, assess their suitability as a Peer Mentor, and approach them with the idea. If they're not interested, nothing is lost. And the best thing about finding a Peer Mentor in these situations is that you already have a common interest – beyond that, the success of your Peer Mentor partnership will

lie in your shared commitment, ability to focus on your goals, and willingness to support each other.

5. The best for last, the world online - These days, we don't even have to leave the house to find tens, hundreds, or even thousands of contacts, friends, or connections to consider as Peer Mentors. Of course, as with all relationships, you must take the time to get to know, like, and trust the one or more people you may have identified as potential Peer Mentors. For example, you may begin as members of the same professional group on LinkedIn, then move to emailing each other directly, then arrange for a one-time Skype call, then more regular Skype calls, and then possibly come up with a project to work on together.

I met Sandy Chernoff online, a consultant and trainer in Vancouver. We connected via LinkedIn, started emailing each other, and then proceeded to a bi-weekly standing Skype appointment. We were both working on writing projects and provided a progress report to each other during those calls. The content of our projects wasn't really important – it was the process that counted. After several conversations, I learned that she was working on an e-learning curriculum, and she learned that I was writing this book. During one call, I committed to finishing two chapters, and she promised to finish three modules of one of her e-courses. We were in a Peer Mentoring relationship, even though we hadn't filled out the 'paperwork' (the Contract in this book).

During the course of our discussions, she introduced me to Dennis K, in Athens, Greece, whose business specialty is LinkedIn Profile makeovers for members. I was interested in perhaps using his services to improve my profile. In the meantime, though, he and I talked via Skype several times and came up with the idea of writing an article together, using a combination of our expertise. It's called "How to Create Influence on LinkedIn;

Keywords and Beyond."[9] We posted the link to my 2,500 LinkedIn connections and to his 13,000, and it's been posted on LinkedIn Pulse and has generated a lot of buzz for us both. We are now brainstorming about a new project we can work on together.

He has not yet done the Profile Makeover for me, but we are now negotiating what resource or skill I can offer him so we can create a more structured Peer Mentor contract with one another. This process has been very informative because we have gotten to know each other better. I learned that he is absolutely always prompt for our calls, takes the initiative in our shared writing tasks, is fair – in fact, generous – about taking credit, and keeps his commitments. These are all qualities I value in a Peer Mentor, so I believe we have a great start.

As in setting goals, once you have in your mind the idea of finding a Peer Mentor, you might see people you meet (or people you already know) in a different light, viewed through the prism of "is this a possible Peer Mentor for me?" You may find yourself more open to the process and perhaps begin a conversation with a likely Peer Mentor. Who knows where it could take you?

---

[9] https://www.linkedin.com/pulse/how-create-influence-linkedin-keywords-beyond-elaina-zuker?trk=prof-post .

9.

Skills Inventory

As we have discussed in earlier chapters, once you begin your Peer Mentor contract, you will want to have specific skills and resources in mind that you can offer or request from each other. The following is a list of "gifts" you may possess, indeed in such abundance that you are willing to offer them to your Peer Mentor; likewise she may also have some of these skills, resources, or abilities to offer you. This list is by no means complete; it is meant only as a starting point to get you brainstorming about your own specific resources. Some of these items may trigger your thoughts and create your own lists. All of these can be useful to put in writing on your actual contract, and in cases where the skill or resource sounds very general, you can break it down into measurable components. For example, suppose one of the skills you bring to the contract is "writing skills." How can you offer those in a way that is measurable to help your partner? Well, you might ask her what is the best way you can help. They might request that you show a sample of a job application letter as a template they can follow. This is a way to make a specific request and offer from a wider skill set.

You can now begin to stockpile the list of skills you bring to the table. Feel free to make notes right on the page, and soon, you'll have your very own personal list (inventory) of skills, resources, and "gifts."

MY TRANSFERABLE SKILLS

I can:

- ▯ Meet deadlines
- ▯ Supervise others
- ▯ Increase sales or efficiency
- ▯ Accept responsibility
- ▯ Instruct others
- ▯ Solve problems
- ▯ Manage money/budgets
- ▯ Manage people
- ▯ Meet the public
- ▯ Organize people
- ▯ Organize/manage projects
- ▯ Research – topic(s) from library/internet sources; interviewing people; finding knowledgeable contacts
- ▯ Manage my time

I have a(n):

- ▯ Ability to delegate
- ▯ Ability to plan
- ▯ Desire to learn & improve
- ▯ Good time management
- ▯ Computer skills
- ▯ Mathematical knowledge and skills
- ▯ Technical Expertise – understanding, interpreting technical manuals, descriptions, re-writing into lay language.
- ▯ Written communications skills

I am:

- ☐ Results-oriented
- ☐ Customer Service-oriented
- ☐ A team player

OTHER TRANSFERABLE SKILLS (DEALING WITH THINGS)

I can:

- ☐ Use my hands
- ☐ Assemble or make things
- ☐ Build, observe, inspect things
- ☐ Construct or repair
- ☐ Follow instructions
- ☐ Operate tools and machinery
- ☐ Drive or operate vehicles
- ☐ Repair things
- ☐ Use complex equipment
- ☐ Repair mechanical devices, equipment, furniture, electrical, or plumbing
- ☐ Design information processes, educational seminars/classes, advertising and PR campaigns

I have:

- ☐ Woodworking skills
- ☐ Computer skills

I am:

- ▯ Safety conscious
- ▯ Good at troubleshooting – finding sources of problems (in mechanical systems, in human interactions)
- ▯ Good with food – cooking, serving, presenting, or giving nutritional information about it

DEALING WITH DATA

I can:

- ▯ Analyze data or facts
- ▯ Investigate
- ▯ Audit records
- ▯ Keep financial records
- ▯ Balance money
- ▯ Calculate, compute
- ▯ Classify data
- ▯ Compare, inspect, or record facts
- ▯ Count, observe, compile
- ▯ Research
- ▯ Handle detailed work – organizing papers, receipts, inventory
- ▯ Develop budgets, create financial systems, maintain records of expenses, payments, or sales

WORKING WITH PEOPLE

I can:

- ▯ Care for
- ▯ Confront others
- ▯ Counsel people
- ▯ Demonstrate something
- ▯ Supervise
- ▯ Speak in public
- ▯ Help others
- ▯ Teach
- ▯ Interview others
- ▯ Anticipate needs
- ▯ Take orders
- ▯ Listen
- ▯ Serve
- ▯ Work with others
- ▯ Negotiate
- ▯ Understand

I am:

- ▯ Patient
- ▯ Persuasive
- ▯ Pleasant
- ▯ Sensitive
- ▯ Supportive
- ▯ Diplomatic
- ▯ Tactful
- ▯ Insightful
- ▯ High energy
- ▯ Open-minded

- Kind
- Adaptable
- Outgoing
- Sensitive to foreign cultures – cultural customs and traditions, languages, cuisine, lodging, and shopping

USING WORDS, IDEAS

I can:

- Articulate
- Innovative
- Communicate verbally
- Be logical
- Remember information
- Research
- Create new ideas
- Design
- Speak in public
- Edit
- Write clearly
- Understand the big picture
- Persuade others to see another point of view
- Create marketing and promotion strategies
- Work on details
- Generate support for ideas
- Listen to, understand, analyze, summarize contents of speech, conversations, interviews, or presentations
- Write proficiently – copyrighting for sales, speechwriting, presentation writing, editing, or technical writing
- Interview effectively – job applicants, guests on talk shows
- Speak, write, and interpret more than one language

LEADERSHIP

I can:

- ▯ Arrange social functions
- ▯ Motivate people
- ▯ Negotiate agreements
- ▯ Plan
- ▯ Delegate
- ▯ Run meetings
- ▯ Direct others
- ▯ Explain things to others
- ▯ Get results
- ▯ Share leadership
- ▯ Think of others
- ▯ Direct projects
- ▯ Solve problems
- ▯ Take risks
- ▯ Empower others
- ▯ Provide nutritional advice
- ▯ Sell
- ▯ Negotiate
- ▯ Influence others to see your point of view
- ▯ Coach – individuals or teams in athletics/fitness; individuals or groups on speeches, media appearances, or court appearances
- ▯ Advise – giving financial counsel or personal advice
- ▯ Counsel – personal/family issues; helping people with personal/career concerns, or educational plans
- ▯ Plan - organization strategies, marketing strategies, fund-raising events, or social events

I am:

- ▯ Decisive
- ▯ Self-motivated
- ▯ A team builder

CREATIVE, ARTISTIC

I can:

- ▯ Dance
- ▯ Perform, act
- ▯ Draw, sketch, or render
- ▯ Present artistic ideas
- ▯ Play instruments
- ▯ Garden
- ▯ Cook, serve, present
- ▯ Organize – ideas, closets, papers, or writing
- ▯ Promote – through social media or one-on-one.
- ▯ Display effectively – ideas in artistic form; pictures for display, photos, art, or visuals for presentation.
- ▯ Style – homes, rooms, or fashion

I am:

- ▯ Artistic
- ▯ Expressive

OTHER

I have:

- ☐ Contacts – in a particular field, industry, organization, city, country
- ☐ Unused (Fallow) Resource – empty apartment, home, office, car truck RV, boat

I know about:

- ☐ Medicine
- ☐ the Law
- ☐ Politics
- ☐ History
- ☐ Economics
- ☐ Travel
- ☐ Foreign Cultures and Customs
- ☐ Foreign Languages
- ☐ add your own areas of knowledge and expertise here

ADD ANY OTHER TRANSFERABLE SKILLS THAT YOU THINK YOU HAVE:

- ☐ ______________________________
- ☐ ______________________________
- ☐ ______________________________
- ☐ ______________________________
- ☐ ______________________________
- ☐ ______________________________

After going through all these skills and resources, you probably have a much larger list than you did before. Highlight the ones that are particularly strong for you and add some notes to describe the specifics of that skill and how you might offer a measurable portion of it to your Peer Mentor. Ask her to do the same. Having assessed and further developed your skills inventory, you will both be well-prepared to work on your Peer Mentor contract and have a wide variety of resources and "gifts" to offer each other towards achieving your separate goals

10.

The Contract

To help you achieve your goal, you need a fellow dreamer, a Peer Mentor to work with you. This Peer Mentor can be a friend, a co-worker, some other close associate, or a complete stranger. Typically, it is better if your Peer Mentor is not your spouse or best friend. Your Peer Mentor need not be a professional (such as a member of clergy, social worker, or counselor) but should be a person who has resources or skills which you do not and who has agreed to support you by sharing their knowledge and skills with you. This is the person with whom you will review your objectives each week, making sure your goals are specific and checking to see if you are sticking to your objectives and eliminating any activities that waste time or energy. In turn, you agree to offer her your support, resources, and skills. I also call this process "re-source-ing" as it is a method for you to use the resources of another person in order to help you achieve your goals.

The contract on the next page is designed for you and your Peer Mentor to organize and formalize your mutual support. This is not a legal document, of course, but in many ways, it can feel more binding than an actual contract, because of your motivation and commitment. In order to start your Peer Mentor relationship off on the right foot, you should:

1. Make copies of the contract so you leave the original blank.
2. Identify one goal (on the left).
3. Write (on the right side) the indicators or measures that will tell you when you have reached your goal.
4. Indicate the resources required in order to achieve your goal.
5. In the "Strategies" section, describe first what you will do for yourself in order to achieve your goal and then what your Peer Mentor will do to support you. Some important ways are indicated (listening, advising), and you can find lists of skills and resources in the previous Chapter.
6. You can give a personal example of how you intend to use each one to support your partner. Photocopy the page and give a copy to your Peer Mentor.
7. Sign each contract. The signing can be the occasion for some personal ceremony (such as during lunch at a special place) that can be repeated when the goals are reached.
8. Agree on specific times to review and renew your contract with your Peer Mentor.

Although you may have many goals you want to work toward, it is important that you choose ONE to begin working on with your partner. It is a new process and having the focus, for each of you, on just ONE of the goals will ensure a successful outcome more quickly. Then, you can both build on that success by choosing another goal to accomplish.

PEER MENTOR CONTRACT

Goal - Desired Outcomes **Indicators/Measures**

____

____

Resources Required: PEER MENTOR will support me by:

____

____

____

____

Strategies:

I will _____ for my Peer Mentor:

- ☐ Listen
- ☐ Advise
- ☐ Share Skills
- ☐ Teach
- ☐ Connect
- ☐ Other

____

____

____

Signed ________________________________ Dated _______

Signed ________________________________ Dated _______

11.

Communication Skills for Success with Your Peer Mentor Contract

Once you create your contract with your Peer Mentor and begin meeting – either in person, via Skype, by email, or on the telephone – there are certain guidelines for the process of communication. The 'what' part of your communication is the content of how you and your Peer Mentor are each progressing towards your goals and the actual sharing of resources with each other. The 'how' of your interactions is the process, the manner in which you communicate various aspects of your ongoing relationship. For example, you may be frustrated with the number of times your partner cancels or shows up late to appointments. Or, you may feel that the amount of time you have devoted to her goal achievement far exceeds the amount of help you have received. Your Peer Mentor may feel the same way in these, or other, aspects of your relationship. Like any good partnership, relationship, friendship, or business alliance, all will not go smoothly all the time. It is important to have a skillful way to express your feelings and describe your expectations to be able to tell your Peer Mentor what you're pleased about and where you feel things are falling short.

FEEDBACK GUIDELINES

Feedback is one way of helping a person change her behavior. It is a way of communicating to a person (or a group) that gives the person information about how she affects others. Feedback helps an individual keep her or his behavior on target and thus better able to achieve her goals. Here are some criteria for useful feedback:

1. It is descriptive rather than evaluative. Describing your own reaction allows the person to use the feedback as she sees fit. Avoiding evaluative language reduces the need for the person to react defensively.

2. It is specific rather than general. Telling a person that she is domineering will not be as useful as telling her that she did not listen to what others said in the most recent meeting, and so others felt forced to either accept her arguments or face attack from her.

3. It takes into account the needs of both the receiver and the giver of feedback. Feedback can be destructive when it only serves one person's needs and fails to consider the needs of the person on the other end.

4. It is directed toward behavior the receiver can do something about. Frustration only increases when a person is reminded of some shortcoming over which she has no control.

5. It is solicited rather than imposed. Feedback is most useful when the receiver, herself, formulates the kind of question those observing her can answer.

6. It is well-timed. In general, feedback is most useful when given at the earliest opportunity after the behavior has occurred depending, of course, on the person's readiness to hear it and the support available from others, etc.

7. It is checked to ensure clear communication. One way of doing this is to have the receiver try to repeat and rephrase the feedback she has received to see if it corresponds to what the sender had in mind.

Feedback is a way of giving help; it is a corrective mechanism for the individual who wants to learn how well her behavior matches her intentions.

HOW TO RECEIVE CRITICISM

Many of us are uncomfortable with criticism. Receiving criticism may make you feel hurt or put down; however, unless you clear up assumptions about others and state what your own needs are, you will repeat unhelpful, and possibly destructive, patterns. Although it's hard to receive, you must remember that criticism can help you in the future. The best way to effectively receive criticism is to really listen to the person assessing you, and to give an assertive back, if necessary. An assertive response to criticism consists of asking for clarification in a firm, calm and direct manner while indicating if you consider the criticism unfair. For example, if your boss says, "This report is inadequate, do it over," your assertive response might be, "I worked hard on this report and think I did a good job. Please explain to me what, specifically, about the report you consider inadequate."

HOW TO GIVE CRITICISM

Giving criticism involves providing negative feedback on someone's work, personal actions, or habits. Criticism, given unassertively or without compassion, may lead you to believe that you have hurt someone's feelings or worry she won't like you. Not giving criticism at all may leave you feeling frustrated, hurt, puzzled, or dissatisfied. In order to give criticism effectively so as not to offend the person you're criticizing and have them hear your complaint and want to change for the future, try to follow these guidelines:

1. Give criticism assertively by being direct and specific. Indicate what the problem is as a statement rather than as a question. For example: "Please do your share of the paperwork. I feel uncomfortable that you leave that part of your daily work so often. I need those figures for my work on a regular basis."

2. Give the criticism as soon as possible after the incident. For example: "I want to speak to you about something that bothered me at the meeting this morning. Can we meet for lunch today?"

3. Make sure your criticism refers to the specific problem rather than the entire person. For example: "I feel angry and upset when you use my ideas at meetings without giving me credit."

4. Try to formulate your criticism in a positive way. For example: "Points x and y should also be included in this report, but otherwise it is very good. I can tell you put a lot of work into this."

Once you get into the rhythm of communication with your Peer Mentor, your relationship should run smoothly and your progress towards your goals will be accelerated.

12.

Conclusion: The Beginning

Now we're at the end of the book, but hopefully, at the beginning of your journey.

I started this book with a simple goal: to create a detailed "how-to" about Peer Mentoring and give readers a step-by-step process to follow if they wanted to use it to get support for their goals.

As I got into the study and the process, I looked into some of the historical and anthropological foundations of barter and reciprocity, gift-giving and exchanges. And of course, the "sharing economy" is all around us – we're either participating in resources like Uber, airbnb, fiverr and so many others, or learn about them via newspapers, Twitter, internet news sites and other sources.

I found all this information fascinating, and decided to include it. I hope you found it interesting as well, learning how it connects ancient practices with the new application of Peer Mentoring.

You may have found and already started working on your goals. You may even have found and begun a contract with a Peer Mentor.

I hope you're as excited as I am about this process and the great catalyst it can be to move you towards accomplishing all you desire in life, work, family, and other categories.

I would love to know how you're doing. How is your trip along this path? What are the successes, the challenges, and the bumps in the road? Perhaps you and your Peer Mentor have decided to improvise, to do a different version of the Contract or the process. I would love to hear about your unique twists and tweaks.

You can write to me at ez4u@ezinfluence.com or visit our website www.ezinfluence.com to view our other books, products and services.

Whatever your goals are, and however you are using your Peer Mentor to achieve them, I wish you the greatest success!

ALSO BY ELAINA ZUKER

Seven Secrets of Influence: Portable Power for the 21st Century

Influence. Everyone Wants It. How To Get It?

Success in today's business world is not dependent just on knowledge which can quickly become outdated or contacts who vanish overnight but an inner resource—the ability to influence. In this highly practical guide, communications expert Elaina Zuker outlines how this essential portable power can be learned, practiced, and mastered to serve whenever and wherever we are.

Influencing is one of the critical business skills required for success today. Strong interpersonal and influencing skills are essential as we work in teams, often across disciplines, and 'sell' our ideas and projects to upper management.

How to Influence People and Win Over Anyone - Audio CD

For just $14.97 and under an hour you can master the same Influence Skills Fortune 500 executives pay $2,000 for at all-day seminars.

Seven Secrets of Influence, the bestselling book (by Elaina Zuker) and corporate seminar has now been condensed into a valuable, user-friendly audio program.

Now, you can get this powerful information in the privacy of your home, office or car.

The Career Success Trilogy:

A Guide to Reawakening Your Dreams and Achieving Your Goals

This dynamic "Success Strategies" series is designed to give guidance, motivation, inspiration plus practical tools and techniques to people who feel "stuck" in their lives and their careers, who are functioning and coping from day to day, but not experiencing much joy, fulfillment, or future-direction.

These simple-to-implement processes ideas give you long range vision plus the knowledge and skills to create a strategy for achieving your goals.

How to reach us:

To engage Ms. Zuker as a speaker or consultant, to book a seminar for your company or organization or to learn how to become a licensed Partner for Secrets of Influence,
visit the website at **www.ezinfluence.com**
or contact us at **ez4u@ezinfluence.com**
or by phone at **514-933-5135**

ACKNOWLEDGEMENTS

I have been the lucky recipient of many “kicks in the can'ts”, mostly from mentors, bosses and teachers, who instilled in me the “failure is not an option” idea, before it was a T-shirt and a corporate slogan.

Of course, I didn't know then about Peer Mentoring, or even thought much about it. Primarily, it was the idea that, with someone in my corner, someone who believed in me, I could develop self-confidence and succeed.

As Brian Schwartz, my talented and wise colleague whose support I will detail later, said when he learned about the concept for my new book: “You know, sometimes I long for my high-school teacher. I work alone, and no one cares whether I tackle that next project or not. I wish I had someone to be accountable to.”

First, I have to acknowledge my optimistic parents, who, despite a difficult reality, always “thought positive” and taught us that every day is a fresh start. My next “swift kick in the can'ts” was from Mrs. Goldberg, my home room teacher in the 9th grade, who told me to quit my back of the room clowning and use my good brain for schoolwork – or else! I never found out what her “or else” meant, but just one withering look from her and all my jokes fell flat.

Alec Fiorentino, my first boss in Montreal, showed me to my desk, gave me an overflowing “inbox” and left town for three days. When I started to ask him what was I to do with certain papers, he said, as he ran out the door, “you'll figure it out, Ms. Zuker.” And somehow, I did! He trusted me with his important work, and I never let him down.

As a young woman, I was hired in San Francisco as the "Girl Friday" to a famous private eye, Hal Lipset. My office was in the drawing room of his 26-room Victorian mansion in Pacific Heights. While this was a great perk, I had no clue about how this business worked. The boss was always away, either out of town on cases, or doing his gumshoe work somewhere in the Bay Area. I was struggling to figure out all the office systems. I kept trying to quit, telling him this "wasn't my field." He said, "I'm successful because I have excellent judgment – you can do this job."

Ellen Jacobsen, one of my first employers in New York, was a very successful public relations woman. She hired me after a 30-minute interview, then assigned me to my first project: organizing the publicity for the launch of the Christian Dior Men's Wear Show at the Hotel Pierre in New York.

I was so new to the city I didn't even know where the Pierre was, let alone who to contact in the press. She gave me lists of things to do every day and encouraged me, and always emphasized that we could not fail! Somehow I pulled it off. She said she never doubted that I could.

One of my first consulting clients, AT & T, hired me at top dollar to conduct training programs for the thousands of women who worked there. I thought I was doing a great job.

One day at lunch the woman who had hired me looked at me, respectfully, and said, "you know, we love your seminar, our people are really learning a lot, your content is so valuable. But , for this kind of top level program, we expect your handouts and materials to be classy and first- rate." They were simply photocopied, stapled packets of notes. She didn't have to tell me this; she was trying to help me keep this important contract. She was giving me a "loving kick in the can'ts".

I hired a graphic designer the next day and poured most of my earnings into creating a beautiful set of participant materials, expensive-looking binders which were up to the standards of this world-class company and its employees.

Most of these supporters were not peers. They were far more experienced and knowledgeable than I was. They were "mentors" in the original sense. They believed in my abilities and were most generous in giving me advice and helping me build my self-confidence.

I have no idea why people believed in my abilities, when I didn't.

I first got the idea of pairing up with a peer as a mentor when my then business partner, Joan Alevras, and I made lists of our different skills and resources. We called our little company "Resources, Inc." and our mission was to help other women identify, access and use their own resources and those of others to achieve success.

We made a pact with each other to support each other in our own separate goals. We called it "Peer Mentoring". We checked in with each other to review our progress. It was comforting to have someone query me about how my efforts were going and to look at the stumbling blocks (often self-inflicted) in my way.

We even called this process "Goal Tenders." Later, I learned that the definition of the terms was different than what we thought it meant, in other words, "you tend my goal and I'll tend yours". It was years later, in fact just a few months ago, that my editor, Ellen Crosby, a Canadian and a hockey fan, pointed out that a "goal tender" means just the <u>opposite</u> of what I thought. It means preventing someone from getting to their goal, which is the opposite of what we were trying to say!

Joan and I have gone our separate ways and I have continued to refine and practice the process we implemented. In the many training programs I conducted (on Influence Skills, Time Management, Business Writing, Team Development) I have taught participants to use the Peer Mentor process as a way to reinforce and refresh their learning from the course.

Twenty years ago, I picked up a used copy of the book "The Gift" by the famous French anthropologist, Marcel Mauss, about the intricate customs and practices of tribes and societies regarding reciprocity, potlatch, the kula and other exotic rituals. I sensed that these customs were a foundational element of the Peer Mentor process.

To my disappointment, the book, translated from the original French, was so dense and academic I couldn't follow most of it.

I kept it though, and thought that one day I would try deciphering it again. It took many years and finding the brilliant Montreal anthropologist, Dr. Gabriella Djerrahian, the author of Chapter 2 of this Book. Gaby, a fluent French speaker has read the book in its original language and was very familiar with Mauss and his seminal work. With her academic discipline, broad knowledge and beautiful writing she brought us this user-friendly understanding of Mauss' work and findings.

In addition to the chapter she wrote, Gaby has been incredibly helpful in the overall conceptual framework for the book, helping me to shape the chapters on Barter and The Sharing Economy, and to elucidate how it all ties into the new concept of Peer Mentoring.

Although she was originally hired to just write one chapter, I think of her more as a collaborator. Her knowledge, insight, enthusiasm and sheer smarts have made this project a joy to work on.

Brian Schwartz of www.SelfPublish.org has been a great supporter. I first met Brian when he converted my book "Seven Secrets of Influence" to an e-book. Since that time, he has expanded his offerings for authors and self-publishers.

From the beginning of this project, he has been a great sounding board and supporter of the idea. With Brian in my corner, I have a great publishing coach by my side.

Through Brian's company, I am so grateful to have met the talented designer, Tatiana Villa, who interpreted the concept to create the beautiful cover design. I especially appreciated her professional and cheerful demeanor, despite my requests for many changes and modifications. Also, the talented and patient

Veronica Yager, who did the beautiful formatting of the interior pages.

When I began interviewing people to edit my manuscript, one CV stood head and shoulders above the rest. Ellen Crosby, an English Major and Graduate Student at McGill University, whose academic credentials were so impressive, complete with all the awards and distinctions (Dean's List, Awards, Scholarships) she had received. I was looking for an editor, and in addition to her academic achievements (and part time jobs to support herself) she had been an editor for several publications in her Nova Scotia hometown as well as in Montreal.

Ellen has far, far exceeded my expectations of a mere copy editor. She has challenged me on consistency, citations and all the other important details which make a tightly constructed and coherent manuscript. Her insights and focus on the big picture have been so welcomed as I struggled through every chapter. It has been a delight to work with her. Watch out world, this young woman is a force to be reckoned with!

Travers Hartnett, my good friend and fellow author (and entrepreneur and Renaissance man) has, from the beginning of this project, been a great sounding board and idea generator. When the book was a tiny seedling, Travers was already thinking outside the box and seeing the entire "garden." I'm so grateful for the gift of his time, friendship and smarts.

And last, but not least, my darling Nancy Lee Havens Vaughn Miller, who has been a dear friend and chief cheerleader for all these years. It seems like yesterday that we spent an entire day in the "Success Department" of Barnes and Noble, reviewing hundreds of titles for format, font and focus. It was clear that this was not going to be "just another self-help book."

Nancy, in her "Executive Vice President, Creative" hat, helped me shape the book within the current context of the business and life environment, helped sharpen my thinking on the audience and positioning of the book, and has been an advisor on every single phase of the process.

Finally, all my students at Montclair State University, who were the first subjects of my early experiments with Peer-Mentoring. They're all grown up and out in the world now, and I'd like to think that they took this helpful model into their careers and life, and are flourishing in whatever they've chosen to do.

Dear reader: I hope you enjoyed
A Swift Kick in the Can'ts - and plan to use some
of its ideas and techniques.

Some of our readers have purchased a second book
as a gift to their Peer Mentor, to get both of you
started on the process.

As you know, we as authors depend on reviews
(like restaurants, Uber and airbnb) from our customers/readers.

If you liked the book, and got value from reading it, would you please take a moment to post your honest review wherever you purchased the book? (Amazon, bookstore, etc.)
It would mean a lot!

Thanks so much, and
Wishing you Much Success!

Sincerely,
Elaina

89354448R00076

Made in the USA
Lexington, KY
26 May 2018